D1135147

FORENSIC QUESTIONS AND ANSWERS
ON THE MMPI/MMPI-2

ALEX B. CALDWELL, Ph.D.

CALDWELL REPORT

Forensic Questions and Answers on the MMPI/MMPI-2
Published 1997 by Caldwell Report

Copyright 1997

To order this book or make inquiries, contact:

Caldwell Report
P.O. Box 24624
Los Angeles, CA 90024

Library of Congress Catalog Card Number: 97-91516

ISBN 0-9620674-1-5

Introduction

This material is for use by both attorneys and forensic psychologists in matters where data from or interpretations of the MMPI or the MMPI-2 are at issue. This paper was first drafted for presentation to a family law conference (hence the extent of material on parenting). It has since been expanded, however, so as to be relevant to the wide range of forensic contexts in which the MMPI and MMPI-2 are utilized.

It is my hope that the material covered will enhance understanding of the test, both to facilitate MMPI-based testimony on direct examination, and, where indicated, its rebuttal on cross examination. For direct examination purposes, an understanding of the basics of the instrument will allow the attorney to better frame meaningful questions. This, in turn, will avoid those awkward moments when the attorney's expert is confused or even bewildered by the meaning of what was supposed to be a friendly question and instead will provide an opportunity for the witness to respond with information that will be helpful to the trier of fact. On cross examination, familiarity with the test allows the attorney to know when the MMPI/MMPI-2 data are being presented in an erroneous, unduly selective, or biased fashion, and this will enable the attorney to formulate better questions to expose this misrepresentation.

MMPI/MMPI-2 data are often important and sometimes vital to the determination to be made by the court in many types of litigation. This merits as much comprehension of the test by the attorney as can be attained in a reasonable amount of time. The following material is relatively condensed and non-redundant. Therefore, it will take a bit of studying (especially the first time through any given section). I expect it mainly to be used as a reference source when a particular topic or question is at issue. Thus, when a deposition is pending, I hope the effort will be well rewarded in the better illumination of fact and opinion and, when at trial, the effective drawing of test implications for persuasion and argument.

Special thanks go to David Shapiro, Ph.D., A.B.P.P. (Baltimore, Md.), for his most cogent and helpful suggestions toward the improvement of an earlier draft of the text. Stuart Greenberg, Ph.D., A.B.P.P. (Seattle, Wa.), generously provided a great many editorial suggestions as well as the list of legal citations at the end of this manuscript. Alice F. Chang, Ph.D. (Tucson, Az.), also provided a wealth of editorial suggestions toward making the text more understandable to a wide range of readers.

QUESTIONS AND ANSWERS ON THE MMPI/MMPI-2

4

QUESTIONS AND ANSWERS ON THE MMPI/MMPI-2

A. THE TEST

A1. What does "MMPI" stand for?

The title of the Minnesota Multiphasic Personality Inventory reflects its origins at the University of Minnesota. It is "multiphasic" in that it provides scores and measurements of a wide variety of aspects of personality. It is a measure of both "personality" and "psychopathology" in that highly elevated scores tell us a great deal about major psychiatric disorders and scores in the "normal range" tell us a great deal about the personality patterns, behaviors, and attitudes of essentially normal adults.

A2. Why "MMPI/MMPI-2?"

The MMPI was first published in 1943 (Hathaway, S. R., & McKinley, J. C., 1943). MMPI-2 designates the only revision of the instrument, which was published in 1989 (Butcher, J. N., Dahlstrom, W. G., Graham, J. R., Tellegen, A., & Kaemmer, B., 1989). The original MMPI has 550 true-false items plus 16 that were repeated for a no-longer-used scoring system (thus a total of 566 items in the standard booklet). The MMPI-2 has 567 true-false items. None are repeated. The acronym "MMPI/MMPI-2" is used to represent the general instrument in its two forms. In those places where "MMPI" is used alone, the reference is usually to the interpretive research literature and clinical experience that are specific to the original instrument.

A3. What does the MMPI/MMPI-2 measure?

Basically the test measures the degree to which the subject answers the items in the same way or in a different way from specific identified groups of people. The more items a person answers the same as the members of an identified group, the more that person is likely to think, feel, and act in ways similar to members of that group. For example, there are 60 items (on the MMPI; 57 on MMPI-2) to which a group of seriously depressed patients consistently responded in a different way from the responses of several groups of non-depressed normals. The items on the test to which the depressed and non-depressed groups responded differently are the items that make up the "depression scale." If a person answers 20 of those items as did the depressed patients, that is actually about average for non-depressed adult subjects. If, however, the person answers 40 of these items in the "depressive direction," there is a great likelihood that that person is thinking, feeling, and acting similarly to the depressed patients and therefore is likely to be very seriously depressed. In this way, the test is basically measuring the similarity of the person's responses to those of each of a variety of groups of people with identified characteristics.

A4. Aren't most of the items quite obvious?

Indeed many items are more or less obvious, e.g., I cry easily," (true) and "My daily life is full of things that keep me interested," (false) are responses that depressed patients make significantly more often than non-depressed individuals. Many items, however, are less obvious (especially when embedded in the context of hundreds of items that may reflect dissatisfaction and unhappiness but are not on the depression scale). For technical purposes in building such scales, it turns out that the content of the item, "what the item says," does not matter much. It only matters that the particular group of people consistently answer the item differently. If the depressed subjects more often say "false" when asked if they ever laugh at dirty jokes, then a false response to this item is scored on the scale whether others recall their having laughed at such jokes or not. This is what is meant by "empirical" item selection.

In addition, the scales are carefully adjusted or "corrected" by items with no obvious relation to the criterion. For example, "I sometimes tease animals," (false) and, "I sweat very easily even on a cool day," (false) proved to be opposite to the responses of patients who were exaggerating their depression. False responses to these items are added to the depression score to balance or compensate for undue self-criticalness and exaggeration.

This is not to say that we are never curious about any of a person's item responses. That one believes he/she is being plotted against, that most of the time he/she wishes he/she were dead, that the person has been in trouble with the law, etc., are statements that are noteworthy and may well merit inquiry in the interview. Various sets of these items have been selected for interview purposes and are called "Critical Items." But for the functioning of a scale and prediction of behavior, it only matters that the particular group of patients consistently answered the items differently.

A5. How many scales are there?

There are 13 fundamental scales. Eight of these are the basic pathology scales or what are referred to as the "clinical scales." Two more are major aspects of personality, and the other three help assess the validity or trustworthiness of all the other scores we have obtained. There are hundreds of other scales and sub-parts of scales (called subscales) that can be scored (Caldwell, 1988, Dahlstrom, Welsh, & Dahlstrom, 1972, Dahlstrom, Welsh, & Dahlstrom, 1975), although the number that get scored on any one person's test is smaller, depending on the clinician (scoring by hand) or the scoring service (programmed scoring by computer).

A6. What are the eight basic "clinical scales" about?

In the order in which they are sequenced from left to right on the profile sheet, their numbers, names, letter designations, and brief descriptions, in the form of the underlying themes and questions asked by the scales, are as follows:

1. Hypochondriasis (Hs). Based on patients who in 1940 were seen as not having a sufficient organic basis for their symptoms, elevations on 1-Hs raise such questions as: How much of the person's mental attention is occupied with problems of bodily malfunctioning? How multiple and diverse are the health concerns that the person presents? To what extent is the person's life oriented toward securing medical care whenever it is perceived to be needed? To what extent does the person forego activities or interests that others think within his/her capacity lest the exertion or stress aggravate his/her physical health problems?

2. Depression (D). How depressed is the person? To what extent or level is the person feeling pessimistic or hopeless, dissatisfied with himself/herself, or persistently unhappy about his/her life and circumstances? The scale can differentiate surprisingly many levels of depression. People with low scores (below the normal adult average) are seen as good-humored and energetic and probably live longer.

3. Conversion Hysteria (Hy). This scale was originally based on a sample of patients characterized by medically problematic pain complaints and other irregular symptoms to which they were seen as showing an unexpected acceptance and indifference. The scale has proved to be a combined measure of two broad aspects: (1) preoccupation with relatively specific somatic symptoms, and (2) a general attitude of avoiding face-to-face conflicts and professing trust and faith in others along with similar socially "nice" and friendly attitudes.

4. Psychopathic Deviate (Pd). Does the person show significant deficiencies of conscience and acts or behaviors that are seen as unsocialized or lacking in recognition of their adverse consequences on others? This scale is a notably complex one. It is the most consistently elevated one in

criminal populations, but it is not a measure of criminality *per se* nor at all limited to such populations. People who get low scores may be seen as loyal and stable but as not having exciting personalities.

5. Masculinity-Femininity (Mf). This is not a "clinical scale;" see below.

6. Paranoia (Pa). Does the person show paranoid trends, and how are they expressed? Elevated scores anticipate a tendency to perceive others as either being "on my side" or "against me." The person with paranoid trends also tends to be rigidly self-righteous, overly sensitive to criticism, and--with more extreme scores--to develop fixed beliefs that he/she is being unfairly treated or persecuted.

7. Psychasthenia (Pt). Is the person a repetitive, obsessive worrier? This is a more one-dimensional scale that measures tendencies to be self-doubting, self-preoccupied, and pervasively anxious. In older usage, an "asthenia" of the psyche was the weakness or inability to resist the obsessive thought or compulsive act.

8. Schizophrenia (Sc). This complex, multidimensional scale was based on a comparison of the responses of groups of schizophrenic patients to those of the relatively normal groups of subjects used in the development of the test. Among other qualities, more extreme scores do measure disruptions of orderly or "linear" thinking, peculiar or bizarre explanations of events (or delusions), and a potential to develop hallucinations (e.g., hearing specific voices outside of oneself talking--often in a hostile way--at you). The scale at intermediate ranges measures self-doubts and the tendency to feel different or alienated from others as well as reflecting the mental confusion that often results from physical insults or other damage to the brain. At milder levels, there probably is some relation to creativity. Low scorers, in contrast, have a solid, balanced, "salt of the earth" quality.

9. Hypomania (Ma). This scale measures tendencies in the manic direction, e.g., toward over-activity, talkativeness, boundless optimism, unrealistic expectations, and a pressured sort of impulsivity (scale 4-Pd assesses a more callous impulsivity). Low scores are particularly meaningful as reflecting a limited or low level of energy that has to be distributed carefully in order to be effective.

10. Social introversion-extroversion (Si). Although the "tenth" scale, it has come to be known as scale 0, and, as with scale 5, it is not a "clinical scale". See below.

A7. Why did you not include scales 5 and 0?

These are basic dimensions of personality but they are not measures of psychopathology per se:

5. Masculine-Feminine (Mf). This scale can most usefully be interpreted as the tendency to orient toward courses of action (a score in the masculine direction) versus orienting toward an awareness of and sensitivity to feelings (feminine direction). Thus, the relatively masculine individual orients more toward doing things, taking action, and dealing with the practical, physical world believing that "actions govern how I feel," and the relatively feminine person orients more toward the appreciation and sharing of subjective feelings, that "how I-- and others--feel governs my relationships and activities." The scores are plotted so that for either sex a high score indicates responding in the direction of the opposite sex.

0. Social introversion-extroversion (Si). High scores reflect shyness, social sensitivity, modesty, and a reticence toward or avoidance of public, social circumstances. Low scores reflect needs for social engagement and a gregarious liking of public, social occasions.

A8. Can the scores be interpreted on the basis of the above descriptions of the individual scales?

In only a very limited way. These descriptions are for understanding the thrust and meaning of the 10 basic scales. Interpretation, however, depends on the *pattern* of the scores. For example, when two scales are higher than any other scale, each may strongly influence how the other is expressed as well as governing the expression of the other less elevated scales. See more detailed comments under Section F, Interpretation, below.

A9. Don't a person's scores change over time?

They certainly do--or there would be no point to treatment or interventions to protect mental health. However, a series of retests on one person will show a strong consistency or persistence of psychological tendencies or traits over time. For example, which two scales are highest (i.e., most elevated or disturbed) may come from among only three of the eight scales across each of the successive retestings. Considerable persistence of scores has been shown across five testings over a 30 year interval.

A10. What are some of the main caveats to appropriate test interpretation in a legal matter?

As powerful and robust as the MMPI is, caution is in order in forming clinical opinions, especially in forensic settings. We have said that a person who answers similarly to another person who is known to be depressed or paranoid is more likely to have the same or similar characteristics. However, that is not the same as saying that we can conclude from the test results alone that the person is necessarily depressed or paranoid. Before we can do so, there are alternative hypotheses that must be ruled out before we can reliably diagnose the person we are currently assessing. Some possibilities are that the scores (1) are the consequences of a deviant approach to the test or "test taking attitude," (2) are the result of incorrect answering due to poor reading comprehension or a lack of attention and concentration, (3) are unduly affected by a transient state or experience not represented in the original test norm groups, or (4) are the result of someone who may answer similarly to a known group but may still be different from them in the real world for no reason other than that the test is not perfect. These questions will be taken up in Section B., Test-Taking Attitude.

CASE NOTES:

14

CASE NOTES:

B. TEST TAKING ATTITUDE

B1. What if the person sets out to slant, distort, bias, or even malinger on his/her responses to the test?

> Everyone has an attitude (or more precisely a set of attitudes) toward being asked such a wide variety of personal questions. The issue then is to understand what attitudes the person had while responding to the items and to adjust our scoring and interpretations accordingly. I will discuss three traditional or basic "validity" scales and then a series of additional scales that further modify our understanding of the person's "test-taking attitude."

B2. What are the three basic "validity scales?"

> L. The scale designated L (sometimes informally called the "lie" scale, but never designated as that by the original authors) is a set of naively defensive items. A high score indicates relatively unsophisticated denial or a more overt guardedness against admitting impulses or behaviors that could reflect badly on one's moral values.

> F. This scale measures the frequency with which the person has made atypical and rarely given responses. These were the true or false responses marked by less than 10% and mostly by less than 5% of normal adults. This score can be elevated by many causes, e.g., severe mental disturbance (genuinely unusual responses), an attempt to fake disturbance, a limited ability to read (misunderstanding the items), being on drugs (confusion), getting mixed up (*i.e.*, out of order) in recording one's responses, or a general lack of sophistication. Which of these may have contributed in the individual case must be determined by the clinician in relation to other scores, the context of testing, and interview data.

> K. This is a subtle correction scale measuring sophisticated minimizing or understatement (high scores) versus undue

candor or self-critical frankness (low scores), whatever their origins. Five of the eight basic "clinical scales" are adjusted upward by some fraction or weight of the person's score on this K scale.

B3. What other scales can expand our understanding of the person's test taking attitudes?

First the commonly scored scales (these three are new to the MMPI-2 and are not available on the original MMPI; see Butcher, J. N., Dahlstrom, W. G., Graham, J. R., Tellegen, A., & Kaemmer, B., 1989):

Variable Response Inconsistency (VRIN): This is a general self-contradiction scale. For example, to say "true" to the item, "most people would lie to get ahead," and later to say "false" to the item, "nearly anyone would tell a lie to keep out of trouble," is to sufficiently contradict oneself as to add one point to the VRIN scale. This serves as a measure of reading comprehension--was the person able to understand the items?--and cooperation--did the person pay attention or just mark answers down randomly?

True Response Inconsistency (TRIN): This is a variant of VRIN structured to detect an "all-true" or "all-false" pattern of responses. To receive a point on this scale, the paired items either must be both marked false or both marked true. For example, the person might say false to the item, "Most of the time I feel blue," and then also say false to the item, "I am happy most of the time." This would count as a false-false self-contradiction.

F-back: This is similar to the rare answer F scale above except that it uses items that fall in the latter part of the booklet (the original F scale being largely from the first half of the items in the booklet).

Different clinicians and different services score their own choice of additional scales. Caldwell Report (Caldwell, 1988) scores several useful scales that most other services do not usually score:

Dissimulation (Ds): This scale measures deliberately faking sick and addresses the general question, "Did the person consciously set out to portray himself/herself as more disturbed than he/she is or to malinger a serious psychiatric illness?" The content of this Ds scale is much more subtle than the F and F-back scales where "what is the rare and atypical response" is consistently obvious. The items on this scale are much more plausible, and they do not have the extreme or psychotic-related item content of the F and F-back scales. Ds overlaps neurotic exaggeration as much as psychotic malingering, and thus it is very helpful in terms of assessing the deliberate exaggeration of a wide variety of symptoms for financial gain or other manipulative intent.

Malingering Positive (Mp): This is a conscious fake-good scale, a very subtle set of items with no consistency of content, i.e., they are not about the same thing. This scale matters greatly in the interpretation of L and K above, e.g., was K elevated because of deliberate defensiveness or was it due to sincere and sophisticated responding? Was L elevated because the person is indeed so morally (and perhaps religiously) proper or because the person was deliberately guarded and unwilling to admit improper behaviors on the test?

Social Desirability (Sd): Very similar to Mp, it adds an element of saying "what a good citizen I am." (There are many different social desirability scales; this is the one developed by J. S. Wiggins, Ph.D.)

Socioeconomic status (Ss): Does the person have an upper class, middle class, or lower class identification with corresponding values and attitudes? This scale matters greatly in interpreting the K scale above. For example, in child custody cases, sophisticated and well educated people of relatively high socioeconomic status may get high scores on the K scale without any degree of conscious deception or of trying to mislead the examiner or the court. They are not being intentionally or consciously defensive, and the adjustments of the scales according to the correction with K should be adequate. In other cases with lower scores on this Ss scale, high scores on K may reflect a deliberate understatement of problems. Low scores on the Ss scale are associated with making unsophisticated or atypical responses; this can lower the K score as well as increasing the elevation on scale F (see above) without any necessary implication of distorted responding or malingering.

B4. What are the subtle and obvious scales, and do they help assess validity?

Five of the eight basic clinical scales (2-D, 3-Hy, 4-Pd, 6-Pa, and 9-Ma) have been divided into "subtle" versus "obvious" subscales with T-scores for each of the five pairs (the average at T-50 with a "standard deviation" of plus or minus 10 T-score points, see section C1 below). One can take the sum of all five obvious T-scores and subtract the sum of the five subtle T-scores to provide a single "obvious minus subtle" or "O - S" index. There is an intuitive expectation that people faking sick will greatly raise their obvious scores but not their subtle scores, and people faking good will raise their subtle scores but not their obvious scores. Although sometimes meaningful, the interpretation of this difference has many complications and qualifications. Some clinicians swear by this "O - S" difference, but most of the MMPI/MMPI-2 experts are either very cautious in using it as a measure of invalidity or reject it outright. Sincerely responding and seriously disturbed patients are much higher in the obvious direction than normal subjects, just as one would expect them to report more obvious distress and symptoms. No three studies on the "O - S" difference have used the same cutoffs since the optimal cutoffs differ greatly from one sample to another.

If a profile seems wrongly called invalid or uninterpretable on the basis of the "O - S" difference, one might ask questions of the sort:

> Do people with genuine disturbances get higher scores on obvious minus subtle subscales than normals do? (Scientifically correct answer: Yes.)

> Is this a large difference? (Yes)

> Do any MMPI/MMPI-2 experts regard "O - S" as a sufficient justification to classify a profile as uninterpretable?

> Who?
>> Dr. Butcher? (No; he rejects it strongly. Did you use his report? And he explicitly rejects "O - S" as a measure of validity?)
>> Dr. Graham? (No.)
>> Dr. Caldwell? (Suggestive at the extreme, not conclusive.)
>> Dr. Greene? (Only at the extreme.)
>> Drs. Friedman, Webb, and Lewak? (Only as a supplement to other indices.)
>> Then who?

> What is your cutoff for calling a profile invalid or

uninterpretable? Who else uses that cutoff? (The cutoffs vary widely.)

Are there any three or more studies that have used (tested, validated) the cutoff you use? (As noted, no more than two studies have used any one, specific cutoff.)

Suppose one had a scale that explicitly measured trying to fake good (or bad)? Suppose there was solid research validating that scale; wouldn't it be better to use that scale? (Overall, the conscious fake-good and fake-bad scales are better than Obvious minus Subtle.)

How can you justify using an index with little if any validation and compromising features when there are validated scale(s) that have been proven to do the task better? (There is no reasonable answer.)

B5. How might I challenge the validity of MMPI/MMPI-2 test results? (This section is in terms of faking good or malingering; the issue of a clinician's interpretive bias will be discussed later.)

For an expert to testify that the MMPI/MMPI-2 results are "wrong", "mistaken", or malingered, then the expert must address the above issues. Some of the questions that need to be answered would be: Was the person conscientious in taking the test, i.e., not repeatedly contradicting himself/herself? If he/she was self-contradictory (more likely in criminal than civil contexts), to what was this due (e.g., low IQ, poor reading skills, carelessness and lack of cooperation, drug effects at the time of testing, etc.)? On what basis do you believe the results should have been different? Why and how much?

What was the self-favorable or self-critical direction of the person's distortion? How do you measure that, or, what scores show that? Did you determine it to be deliberate or could other factors account for it, e.g., being very sophisticated, or naively moralistic, or genuinely disturbed? How extensive was the distortion?

CASE NOTES:

22

<u>CASE NOTES:</u>

C. THE PROFILE

C1. What do all those numbers mean?

Since a person can be relatively more deviant on one scale than on another, we need a method to represent this: which scales are the most deviant and which are less so?

Mean and standard deviation: The mean score on a scale represents the average score of all of the normals taking the test (within the "normative" group). The standard deviation expresses the extent to which the scores are spread out or bunched together. For the MMPI and MMPI-2, these are fitted or "transformed" so that however many items is the average normal raw score on a scale is placed at 50 on the graph or "profile," that is, "T-50" corresponds to the normal adult average on each of the scales. The standard deviation is set at 10 points. A transformed score of 60 (i.e., "T-60") is then one standard deviation higher than average, "T-70" represents two standard deviations above average, etc. When psychologists using the MMPI or MMPI-2 refer to "T-scores," they are referring to these Transformed scores. These transformations are used primarily so that one may speak of scale elevations that are comparable from one scale to the next. One cannot do that with the raw scores because having a raw score of, say, 15 responses on a short scale might reflect an unusuallly high score where 15 would be a quite low score on some of the longer scales. (For comparison purposes, with IQ scores the overall mean raw score or average score is placed at 100, and on the Wechsler Adult Intelligence Scale-Revised [WAIS-R] the standard deviation is set at plus or minus fifteen IQ points.)

C2. What on earth does a psychologist mean by "the MMPI code?"

This is simpler and less occult than it sounds. We simply

rank order the T-scores from the most elevated scale to the second most elevated to the third, etc. It turns out that people who have the same two scales most elevated are consistently similar to each other. We then use the numbers that are paired with each scale (see above); for example, if the fourth scale (Pd) is the highest of all and the ninth scale (Ma) is second, we will say the person obtained a "49 profile." The person is thus classified as fitting or belonging to the "49 code type," simply because the fourth and ninth scales are rank-ordered highest and second highest. We then base our descriptions and predictions on the identified characteristics of subjects who have obtained this pattern, with modifications and elaborations according to which other scales are somewhat less elevated or perhaps notably low and unelevated.

Once in a while a profile may be defined by a solitary spike on one scale, e.g., scale 9 (Hypomania, Ma). Other profiles may be defined by a set of three scales (or, rarely, four scales). It is the responsibility of the psychologist interpreting the MMPI or MMPI-2 to be familiar with these "codes" and what they mean behaviorally.

C3. What is "the profile?"

References to "the MMPI-2 profile" are to the standard graph. This provides a visualization of the array of scores on the 13 basic scales. If the average or "mean" raw scores for normal subjects are all plotted at the "T-50" line with a standard deviation of ten (the raw score corresponding to one standard deviation above normal being plotted on the T-60 line), then a "normal range" can be defined. On the MMPI this was set as being less than two standard deviations different from the mean, i.e., less than T-70 and more than T-30. For the MMPI-2 this classified too many disturbed patients as being "in the normal range," and the upper cutoff was adjusted to T-65 (i.e., one and one-half standard deviations). On the

MMPI-2, therefore, any Transformed or "T" score at 65 or higher is considered clinically significant or statistically "abnormal."

C4. Does "T-70" mean the 70th percentile?

No: such an assertion should be a bright red flag to the attorney since it reflects a major misunderstanding of the relation of percentiles to more or less "normally distributed" or "bell curve" data. Percentiles are easily misleading. The difference in raw scores between the 50th and 55th percentiles is very small due to the bunching of raw scores at the middle of the curve (only a few items will "move you past" the scores of many other persons). The difference in raw scores between the 90th and 95th percentiles is much larger due to the stretching out of raw scores at the ends of the curve (e.g., it takes many more items to get from the 90th to the 95th percentile than from the 50th to the 55th). The statistical issue is that with more or less "normally distributed" data, differences in percentiles reflect differences in raw score performance quite poorly. Differences in one's position on a normal curve, the T-scores, are far more comparable in terms of differences in performance.

On the MMPI the percentiles for the same T-score varied somewhat from scale to scale. For all of the eight basic clinical scales on the MMPI-2, however, T-70 corresponds to the 96th percentile. Thus, any misattribution of percentile value according to the T-score number immediately calls for cross examination or rebuttal.

CASE NOTES:

26

CASE NOTES:

D. WHICH IS THE BETTER TEST TO USE, THE MMPI OR THE MMPI-2?

D1. At what ages can one use the MMPI or MMPI-2? What about the adolescent form, the MMPI-A?

> The original MMPI has been extensively researched from age 15 upward. There is no upper ceiling on age except capacity to respond. The MMPI-2 was intended for age 18 upward. A subsequent version (with more extensive changes) was designated MMPI-A (Archer, 1992) for use with adolescents age 14 through 17 (MMPI-A if 18 and living at home; MMPI-2 if 18 but not). This MMPI-A revision has posed many problems; for example, by comparing adolescents to other adolescents, they mostly look normal even when their behavior is seen to be seriously problematic. I (e.g., Caldwell, 1990, 1996) advocate using the MMPI-2 booklet together with the MMPI profile from about age 15 on up because I feel it better predicts adolescent behavior; my computer interpretation system has a great many internal adjustments for such younger age levels (based on the extensive MMPI research on adolescents). I have seen valid tests at ages 13 and 14, but many items have adult points of reference; at this age level the youngster needs to be relatively bright and verbal. Others disagree with me on this issue and prefer the MMPI-A below age 18 because the items and age norms are tailored for adolescents. This is an open and not easily resolved question. Either choice (MMPI-A or MMPI-2 at or below age 17 or 18) can be defended as well as attacked.

D2. Can one choose and defend the MMPI booklet versus the revised MMPI-2? How about the different sets of norms?

> As of this writing (1996), most psychologists have switched from the MMPI (the original set of questions) to the revised MMPI-2. Some have held out for the original MMPI because they are familiar with the established meanings of the

patterns. Again, both positions can be defended, and both have problems. One problem with the original MMPI is the dated wording; the MMPI-2 items are clearly more "user friendly" in that many awkward, out-of-date, sexist-worded, and other problematic items in the MMPI have been reworded or eliminated. These item changes seem to make much less difference for subjects beyond age 50 to 60 for whom the original idioms are familiar, and here the MMPI would be an equally justifiable option.

The group of normal subjects from whom the MMPI norms were derived were virtually all Caucasian and living in Minnesota. Many in this test-development sample were from farms although many others were urban. This "lack of current representativeness" ("based on just a bunch of farmers, wasn't it, doctor?") is probably not as much of a problem as it might initially seem in that a considerable part of the U. S. population in 1940 was still living on farms. The socioeconomic level (see Section B3 regarding scale Ss) is what matters the most, and the original sample was appears minimally biased in this regard. Also, for technical reasons the original means were somewhat in error so that the average profiles for all subsequent groups of normal subjects have been at least mildly elevated on the MMPI. The major advantage of using the MMPI profile (rather than the MMPI-2 profile) is that there exists 50-plus years of research on the codes or patterns discussed above and subsequently; pattern interpretations have a much greater interpretive meaningfulness from the MMPI profile than from the MMPI-2 profile.

The normative sample for the MMPI-2 was broadly representative of the U. S. population in terms of geography, age, and racial-ethnic membership (Butcher, J. N., Dahlstrom, W. G., Graham, J. R., Tellegen, A., & Kaemmer, B., 1989). Unfortunately, they used volunteers who were of a much higher level of education and socioeconomic status than the

U. S. population, and this had selective effects on various scales (especially scales F and K as noted above and in relation to the Ss scale). The lower the person's socioeconomic status, the more misleading the revised T-scores are likely to be. Another disadvantage is that the new "codes" on the MMPI-2 profiles look the same but are not; that is, the group of people who get a "49" code on the MMPI is only partly the same group as those who get a "49" code on the MMPI-2. Some codes identify almost exactly the same groups of people, but other codes identify quite different sets of people (for a detailed discussion, see Caldwell, 1997).

D3. Can one set of raw scores be recorded or plotted on both the old profile and the new profile?

Yes: a single set of raw scores can easily be plotted on both profiles without doing any injustice or violence to their meaning. Whether or not we need to do this is a current controversy in the personality assessment journals; most authors are arguing that the two different ways of looking at the scores lead to substantially different conclusions about the person, and a few are dismissing the differences as inconsequential. Caldwell (1997) among others argues that by far the most meaningful way to interpret the scores from the MMPI-2 is by also plotting the MMPI-2 raw scores on the original MMPI profile; this gives us access to the 50-plus years of MMPI research while allowing use of the updated and improved MMPI-2 booklet.

A psychologist interpreting *only* the MMPI-2 profile should be aware of this problem and able to explain how he/she is compensating or allowing for it. If the code (two highest scales) changed from MMPI-2 to MMPI or there were other obvious shifts in the "T-scores," the psychologist could be asked: (1) Is there published research on this particular pattern (code type) on the MMPI-2? (almost none) (2) Would this set of raw scores yield a different pattern if you were to plot them on the original MMPI? (3) Would an MMPI pattern or code that was different from this MMPI-2 pattern change your interpretation? (4) What would those changes of interpretation be? What else?

CASE NOTES:

CASE NOTES:

E. ADMINISTRATION OF THE MMPI/MMPI-2

E1. Can any adult be given the MMPI or MMPI-2?

> Taking the test requires, of course, a minimum reading level. For the MMPI (Hathaway & McKinley, 1943) this was considered to be sixth grade or sometimes fifth grade. For the MMPI-2 (Butcher, J. N., Dahlstrom, W. G., Graham, J. R., Tellegen, A., & Kaemmer, B., 1989), this was originally considered to be eighth grade but some have argued that a sixth grade reading level is sufficient. It appears that there are only a very few items that are more difficult than characteristic for a sixth grade reading level. Discussing the items with the person taking the test is strongly discouraged (even though occasionally necessary if intelligence or reading level are limited) since it is very difficult to explain an item without influencing the person's response to it. The test administrator will have his/her own understanding of the item, and this can easily influence the explanation; an important aspect of the test is that everyone has their own interpretations of the items. The best testing situation is clearly to allow the person to interpret each item his or her own way.

E2. Can the test be read to the patient?

> As just indicated, this is to be avoided if possible. Some more or less illiterate subjects can hear and understand the items adequately but not read them. Here, some measurement is usually be better than none, and under such duress it would be justified to read the items to the subject out loud. An audiotape is available for this purpose, although the tape repeats each item (in a droning voice in order not to influence the subject), and this takes a longer period of time to complete. For foreign subjects there are translations of variable quality into many languages. The use of a translated form is, of course, preferable where the person's reading

comprehension in English is limited or absent, and the person is literate in the other language.

E3. Can the person take the booklet and answer sheet home with them and complete it there?

> This question is highly problematic. It is officially discouraged but not explicitly forbidden (American Psychological Association, 1992; American Psychological Association, 1994). This is not unreasonable in a clinical setting where the therapist knows the client, particularly if the client lives alone or can be trusted to take the test alone. It is hard to imagine a forensic evaluation circumstance in which this would be acceptable, although this might be defensible in special or unique circumstances (e.g., very stringent time limits and no other possible way to obtain the test). It would need very careful explanation and justification in the report and testimony as to what assurances the examiner could trust that no one else had influenced the person's responses. Even completing the test in a waiting room with others present is to be discouraged, and, in general, it should never be done in the presence of family members.

CASE NOTES:

34

<u>CASE NOTES:</u>

F. INTERPRETATION

F1. Does the test tell us about essentially normal people as well as people who are seriously disturbed?

> Yes: the MMPI/MMPI-2 scales range from below the normal adult average to highly elevated scores. Quite low scores reflect mostly positive attributes in contrast to high scores which reflect moderate to severe psychological and emotional problems. Nevertheless, for discussion purposes, let us divide this between profiles that are in the statistically "abnormal range" (one or more of the eight "clinical scales" are at or above T-70 on the MMPI or at or above T-65 on the MMPI-2) versus "normal range" profiles where the eight "clinical scales" are all below those cutoffs.

F2. What do elevated and disturbed profiles tell us?

> The original intent in developing the MMPI was to measure levels of psychopathology, to remove some of the guesswork and opinionation from judging the severity of psychiatric disorders. Patients seen by psychologists and psychiatrists *mostly* have profiles in the disturbed or abnormal range. The mostly is important because a minority do not. For various reasons--mainly expectations about how the test will be used--even some hospitalized psychiatric patients do obtain "normal range" profiles. Often these are evidently defensive (or paranoid), and a few of these profiles would be seen as uninterpretable or invalid. A few people are hospitalized to treat specific symptoms or due to special situations (e.g., severely adverse living circumstances) who are not seriously disturbed, and their profiles may be valid and within the "normal range."

> As noted in the discussion of profiles and codes above, the pattern of scores can tell us a great deal about the kinds of emotional problems with which the person is struggling. For

example, the MMPI patterns may tell us how these problems will be presented, to what degree they are crippling to the person, perhaps what are the typical origins of such problems, what diagnoses most often go with the pattern, how serious a suicidal risk may be, which medications are likely to help (or not likely to help), what is the risk of chemical abuse and dependence, what psychotherapeutic interventions are likely to be of benefit, etc.

Expertise in these patterns or code types requires considerable training and experience. For example, has the person had course work in personality measurement and test interpretation specifically (psychiatrists rarely have)? Under whom has the person trained? How extensive was that training or supervision (just one or two one-day or two-day workshops ever)? How many profiles is the person called on to actually interpret per week (or month or year)? About how many has the person ever interpreted? Has the person ever published research that used the MMPI or MMPI-2?

F3. What do "normal range" profiles tell us?

Qualitatively, the behavioral tendencies and emotional dispositions measured by the MMPI/MMPI-2 scales change very little between the "normal" and "abnormal" ranges. Rather, the changes are mostly in terms of the range of symptoms, their severity, and the general level of impairment. For example, if scale 2-D-Depression is markedly elevated, one might talk about deep pessimism, feelings of hopelessness, a slowing of reactions, or morbid preoccupations (which characteristics would also be influenced by which other scales are concomitantly elevated). If the score is mildly elevated but in the normal range, one would consider such words as serious, earnest, sensitive to criticism, or self-dissatisfied (but not necessarily "depressed"). Scores below the normal average would suggest such terms as alert, energetic, humorous, laughterful, self-confident, and perhaps willful or uninhibited. Thus, the words used to describe the behaviors change much more than do the underlying qualities or behavioral potentials being measured.

The profile patterns or code types in the normal range essentially identify stylistic patterns, for example, inhibition and politeness vs. assertiveness and outspokenness, responsible vs. irresponsible, unusual attitudes vs. social conformity, restless vs. easygoing, socially outgoing vs. shy or restrained, modest vs. showing off, normal or mildly heightened response to physical illness vs. indifference or carelessness about health, tendencies to take advantage vs. to be "used" by others, etc. The supplemental scales are very helpful in this range to qualify and elaborate these emotional orientations, e.g., highly productive versus struggling to keep things organized, upward status striving vs. drifting downward, rigidity vs. flexibility of values, emotional restraint vs. expressiveness, an ability to put up a deceptive facade vs. a lack of self-awareness, etc. Thus, in this range it becomes a "personality" test rather than a "psychopathology" test. (Whether or not psychiatric illnesses are discrete categories, "you have it or you do not," or are primarily continua--which latter I strongly contend they are--is a complex and unresolved argument not for elaboration here, except to point out the example of the extended continuum of depression discussed above.)

F4. Do such factors as litigation, indictment, or imprisonment affect the interpretation of a person's responding to the MMPI/MMPI-2?

This is a difficult and complex question that is often actually or potentially at issue. Although the answer is clearly "yes," the effects are highly variable from one individual to another. We will first look at it at the test item level, considering criminal and civil implications separately, and then consider the question in terms of the pattern of scores, again at both the criminal and civil levels. It would almost always be informative to have a prior and ideally non-distressed MMPI/MMPI-2 with which to compare the current testing, but this is rarely available. When one or more previous testings do happen to be available, a detailed comparison (which I have frequently been asked to dictate) can be highly instructive as to the person's emotional and psychological changes over time.

At the criminal level, especially if the person finds himself/herself in jail, many likely changes "jump out" at us. A true response that "someone has it in for me," may well be the District Attorney; the prosecution says "insulting and vulgar things about me;" jail *is* a "strange and peculiar" experience; etc. A person might well wonder about a prisoner's assertion that his sex life is satisfactory. Nevertheless, however much one felon may dislike the D.A., he may feel that the (so-and-so) is simply doing his job and not respond to the persecutory items, whereas another felon may feel personally and diabolically plotted against and say so on the corresponding MMPI or MMPI-2 items. A project is under way at the time of this writing (at Dr. David Shapiro's urging) to provide a listing of likely incarceration-affected items that any given individual answered in the "scored direction" in order to help the clinician to allow or compensate for the effects of imprisonment.

The expectations of item changes in civil litigation appear more varied, depending on what is at issue. For example, one might anticipate an excess of somatic complaint items in a personal injury suit or in many workers' compensation litigations; one might expect an exaggeration of depression in some kinds of suits over personal losses and damages; or one might not be surprised to see changes in responses to items about unfair treatment by a person involved in a divorce action or in child custody litigation. As to the latter, one client might say, "Of course, my ex and his/her attorney are plotting against me!" while another may feel, "He/She is just saying what his/her attorney told him/her to say." It is always at least a little more uncomfortable when the custody litigant does make the persecutory response as compared to when someone who, in similar circumstances, does not. But in any case, the weight of proof from a single item is very weak; it *can* be no more than a hasty, careless, or misread entry.

The "second level" of consideration is of the changes in the *pattern* of scores and in the elevation (severity) of an MMPI/MMPI-2 profile. In the criminal context one commonly relies on the complex of validity scales to answer such questions as: Was the person self-consistent in his/her responses (see VRIN and TRIN above)? Was there an excess of atypical responding (scales F and F-back)? Was the fake-sick (Ds or Dissimulation) scale unduly elevated? Was the amount of "psychotic" responding on the test contradictory to the absence of any apparent evidence of psychosis in the interview? Or, in contrast, were the severe elevations due to genuine psychosis and/or to limitations of reading comprehension and intelligence rather than exaggeration or malingering? The wording of the Caldwell Report narrative interpretations is often intended to delineate such ambiguous alternatives that require clinical discrimination to answer. The "actuarial report" (see sections G3 and G4) can only reflect what the person said and what behaviors are typical for the scores obtained; ambiguities in the scores must be resolved by clinical evaluation.

A central intention of Hathaway in the original development of the MMPI was indeed to measure personality change over time; we expect both internal and circumstantial changes to affect the person's pattern of scores. A criminal indictment that is experienced as life-devastating may plunge a person into a major depression (or even--rarely--suicide) with pervasive effects on his/her test item responses and scores. Thus, there can be major changes of scores due to the broader social and interpersonal relationship consequences of an indictment or to the loss of freedom due to imprisonment that are not necessarily item-specific to the individuals and events of being prosecuted or imprisoned. There is also a fairly common response-to-imprisonment depression that usually is transitory; this is typically an episode of depression that lasts perhaps several weeks or a few months (the duration is variable) which then subsides as the person becomes adjusted to the changed circumstances or perhaps reverts to a pattern of not caring much what happens to him/her.

Changes of MMPI/MMPI-2 scores and patterns in civil cases appear, as with the item changes, to be much more variable and dependent on the circumstances. The fake-sick (Ds or Dissimulation) scale seems relatively effective across a variety of contexts of overstatement and malingering, including somatic exaggeration, such as may occur in cases involving physical injury. The Depression scale contains eleven items (MMPI; nine items on the MMPI-2) that were not included in the scale because they discriminated depressed patients from normals but only because they discriminated truly depressed patients from patients exaggerating their depression. These internal adjustments seem to work quite well (and they are in contrast to depression scales such as the Beck that have no such adjustments, are quite obvious in their item content, and are far more open to challenge as to malingering).

Child custody profiles are a special case. Here the balance of scores between the "conscious fake-good" scales and the score on the scale measuring socioeconomic status identification can be crucial. For example, is this profile relatively normal due to a deliberate or even extreme effort to "look good," or is it a valid profile reflecting a sophisticated and sincerely self-favorable presentation? Or, given that they are not mutually exclusive, was it a mixture of both? See section B3 for a more detailed discussion of these scales.

In many contexts it appears that the *pattern* of scores reflects the person's style of self-protection, the person's defense mechanisms, avoidances, and ways of compensating. The *elevation* of the scores reflects the relative severity or urgency of such defenses at the time of testing. Repeated testing over a stressful time interval will typically show this as a rise and fall of the profile elevation, and a similar pattern is frequently obtained each time despite these changes of elevation. Thus, it would be expected that the person's profile obtained in the midst of child custody contention would be more elevated than it would have been at some prior time of greater affection and equanimity, but the pattern of scores is likely to be similar (e.g., the same two scales are highest both times, the scales ranked first and second become first and third, or there is a similar, overlapping shift). Thus, the stress of custody litigation is more likely to change the elevation (urgency) of the person's defenses than the pattern of those self-protective mechanisms; most often it exacerbates them rather than altering them.

In terms of predispositions, the question could be asked, is there "a litigious profile" on the MMPI/MMPI-2? The answer is between yes and no. Essentially, there is a cluster of non-psychotic paranoid profiles where there appears to be a substantial increment in the readiness to file lawsuits, appeal administrative decisions, or otherwise litigate. Frequently there is a denial of personal, retaliatory intent with instead a self-righteous sense of having to stop the person or group from hurting *other* people. This cluster is composed of scale 6-Pa in combination with several other scales. One is the combination of the paranoid scale with an elevation on the depression scale 2-D (the "26/62 code"). This is marked by a resentful martyrdom where the person feels forced to sue to restore his/her lost or damaged rights. Scale 6-Pa combined with scale 3-Hy (the "36/63 code") is the maximally self-righteous pattern; it would be wrong to let a wrong go unchallenged. Perhaps the most litigious pattern of all is the combination of 6-Pa with scale 4-Pd, the MMPI pattern (the "46/64 code") that strikingly fits the formal psychiatric diagnosis of paranoid personality. Often a petty tyrant in the home (threat of loss of control over his/her temper), the person finds acquiescence of his/her own will to be intolerable, and one lawsuit after another may be "necessary" to protect his/her rights or correct the wrongdoing of others. The combination of scale 6-Pa with scale 9-Ma (the "69/96 code") marks an energized vigilance against mistreatment by others, and "obvious" or public mistreatment can easily leave one with "no choice" but to sue. This common tendency across these paranoid patterns to file suit over unfair or wrongly hurtful treatment operates when the profiles are in the normal range as well as when they are "abnormally" elevated. As scale 6-Pa is increasingly elevated (more intense paranoid trends), the pressure to litigate is seen by others as driven by the person's internal needs and private logic, and the suits become less and less realistic.

In terms of consequences, a contrasting question could be phrased, is there an MMPI profile that is the effect or result of being in litigation, child custody or otherwise? There is, after all, considerable consistency in the custody litigant patterns involving combinations of scales 3-Hy, 4-Pd, and 6-Pa (see the detailed discussion of scale combinations 34/43, 36/63, and 46/64 in section H3.). The point here is that having one of these patterns, even at a quite unelevated level, marks a predisposing vulnerability to become litigious when one feels seriously demeaned or betrayed. Then if and when things go wrong and litigation ensues, the defenses go up (i.e., profile elevation increases), but at least in most cases the pre-existing styles of personal denial, emotional egocentrism, and/or judgmental blame appear more to be accentuated than newly generated by the process of litigation.

In any given case, the evaluation of the various effects of litigation and imprisonment on the individual versus the contribution of pre-existing tendencies is a matter of judgment by the forensic expert. This is a difficult and sometimes arbitrary distinction between changes that are (1) solely because of the forensic circumstances, (2) aspects of the profile that reflect overall emotional shifts, and (3) the interaction between litigation or incarceration *and* the person's emotional state. For example, the question, "Is this a chronically depressed person or is it someone who only gets transitorily depressed when his/her freedoms are taken away?" is best answered by an integration of the MMPI/MMPI-2 data with the person's history, e.g., the circumstances of any previous depressions. The same is true for the question, How much of a belief that one is being plotted against is a function of the situation alone versus an increase or exacerbation of a longstanding tendency to overly classify others as either allied with or hostile and threatening toward oneself? The key element in this determination is whether the attitudes and emotional states reflected in the MMPI/MMPI-2 results are consistent with the person's prior history or reflect a substantial emotional and behavioral change. Do these results match what we know of the person's prior conduct and expressions of feeling? Or, are these results discrepant from or inconsistent with those prior actions and attitudes? This match versus mismatch is then the fundamental basis for assessing the consequences of the circumstances of litigation and/or imprisonment on the personality makeup indicated by the MMPI/MMPI-2.

F5. Can the risk of dangerousness be assessed with the MMPI/MMPI-2?

A great many factors have been shown to be related to the risk of violent and dangerous behaviors. For example, Steadman et al. (Monahan and Steadman, 1994, p. 303) list 37 different potential risk factors. In line with common thinking about the problem, they group these into four general categories or "cue domains." These are: 1. Dispositional

Factors such as age, gender, social class, various aspects of long-term personality style, and intellectual functioning including neurological impairment. Their second, Historical Factors, includes family history (rearing, abuse, deviance), work history, education, mental hospitalization history, and history of crime and violence. Their third domain is of Contextual Factors including perceived stress, various aspects of social support, and means for violence (having guns, etc.). Fourthly, they list Clinical Factors including symptoms (delusions, hallucinations, etc.), personality disorder diagnoses, level of functioning, and substance abuse. The first two categories of factors are not considered amenable to change or management, but the second two are. For purposes of forensic evaluation and testimony, these constitute a very comprehensive checklist of items to consider. There are, however, no formulas as yet as to how to weigh all of these in an individual adjudication. At least relative weights should be forthcoming as their MacArthur Risk Assessment Study develops.

For present purposes, I would like to offer my own understanding of how the MMPI/MMPI-2 fits into a forensic evaluation of the risk of violence and dangerousness. This applies both to the consideration of a previous act, perhaps the charge of an indictment, as well as in evaluating a decision to release or continue incarceration. I emphasize this is my own structure and not an attempt to represent the consensus of thought in the field (which is better reflected in the multi-correlational approach of Steadman et al.). I offer this as my attempt to clarify and facilitate our thinking about this issue within court settings that must continue making decisions on available information as to the adjudication of past violence and to assess the risks of restraining particular individuals or not.

A distinct subset of the patterns or "code types" on the MMPI has disproportionately often been associated with past histories of aggressive acts as well as occasions of violent behaviors that precipitated professional contact. This subset of patterns accounts for a substantial proportion of prison inmates. In contrast, for other MMPI patterns (e.g., those seen in medical settings) such behaviors are notably rare. The following section discusses the contrasting questions, what predictions do I believe can legitimately be made, and what are the limitations on how much can be predicted?

I propose three points of focus. The first is the psychological *threshold* for aggression and violence: how much is it likely to take to elicit a violent or dangerous reaction from this individual? The second is the array of moderator variables that influence the likelihood of violence such as sex, age, poverty, the availability of guns and alcohol, and the presence or absence of constructive social support. The third is the important but never specifically predictable contribution of circumstantial precipitants or provocations, elements I call the "stage setting" and the "immediate trigger" to a violent outburst.

The primary relevance of the MMPI/MMPI-2 is obviously to the first of these, the assessment of the aggressive threshold of the individual. As a measure of a person's emotional state and behavioral tendencies at a point in time, the MMPI/MMPI-2 actually overlaps each of Steadman et al.'s four categories. It is not only an indication of the person's clinical status, but it is also strongly influenced by the person's long-term personality makeup and emotional history. The pattern and severity of a profile reflect both the effects of past traumatic experiences on the personality makeup as well as their activation by ongoing contextual threats and pressures. In particular, the high risk patterns on the MMPI are strongly associated with histories of physical and/or sexual abuse, some more with one or the other, so that "past abuse begets present and future abuse" is strongly reflected in these patterns.

MMPI patterns dominated by the following four scales are those most indicative of potential dangerousness. Most crucial throughout the research literature are the failures of conscience and the capacity for indifference or callousness toward others that are associated with primary (highest in the code) or otherwise substantial elevations on scale 4-Pd (psychopathy). Emotional pressures and abrupt losses of self-control are strongly energized by elevations on the manic scale, 9-Ma. Elevations on scale 6-Pa (paranoia) particularly add to unreleased resentments and to the urgency to retaliate or counterattack when unfairly and unduly provoked. Elevations on scale 8-Sc (borderline-schizoid-schizophrenic; especially when elevated in conjunction with one or more of these three other scales) strongly add to the meanness or even sadism of the aggression expressed as well as to the displacement of aggression or violence onto "wrong" targets (e.g., remotely or accidentally involved people). Thus, if there is a combination of these scales, that is, the profile is coded (i.e., the scales are rank-ordered) as "489," "64," "98," "846," etc., then the risk of dangerousness is far greater than if the profile is characterized by elevations on inhibitory scales (e.g., 2-D and/or 1-Hs). Relatively feminine scores on scale 5-Mf in males and elevations on shyness or 0-Si in either sex also have demonstrated inhibitory effects on the risk of juvenile delinquency as well as being inhibitory in clinical experience with adult legal offenders. In addition, validly normal profiles are consistently less often associated with dangerousness than are elevated and disturbed profiles.

There are other elements to the aggressive threshold that the MMPI/MMPI-2 does not assess. Some of these are better reflected in other psychological tests such as those tapping violent imagery. In some cases, damage to brain function can unblock aggressive or even assaultive behavior. Also, impaired educational achievement and limited job skills can be damaging to the person's self-esteem and tolerance of frustrations.

The longer-term moderator variable factors significantly affect the risk of violence over time. Men are far more often violent than women. Violence drops off considerably after age 40. Alcohol contributes greatly to losses of judgment and control in a wide range of contexts from the abusive punishment of children to homicide. The frustration of chronic poverty with "nothing to lose" alters the threshold of aggression as can persecution on a racial or ethnic basis. A history of chronic interpersonal estrangement, an absence of any warm and caring attachments, and "forever provocative" relationships raise the level of frustration and the likelihood of aggression. Conversely, a steady job, sobriety, loving relationships, and caring and constructive social support (more than one wants to lose) operate to lower the probability of dangerous aggression.

I believe that the precipitating circumstantial factors can be divided broadly into what I would call "stage setting" and "immediate trigger" elements. By stage setting I mean recent deteriorations in the person's circumstances that significantly raise the level of frustration. This would include such turns of events as the souring of a relationship into acute conflict and rejection, monetary setbacks (e.g., loss of a job), public insults to one's reputation, abandonment by those who matter, and the defeat of a personal expectation. Many occasions of violence seem to follow serious downturns in the person's life, a phase when previously tolerable frustrations have subjectively escalated into major aggravations. The MMPI/MMPI-2 is of secondary relevance here in that it will often suggest what areas will be most sensitive to the person and what will be more rather than less upending to him/her. The contribution of these stage setting changes is, of course, a matter of clinical evaluation and expert opinion, and they may be difficult to ascertain because the downturn events often have no direct or obvious relation to the outburst.

The second and directly evocative aspect of circumstantial

factors is the "immediate trigger" which may be reconstructed but cannot be predicted. A policeman with a *very* unelevated "98" profile was an excellent, energetic officer for three years until a long-haired kid spit on him in a very public setting; the enraged beating of the adolescent was his instant firing. I had hesitated to recommend him for initial hiring because of just this kind of remote possibility; ironically the excellence of his performance validated the normality of his profile while the unfortunate episode validated the behavioral potential of his pattern when under (for him) *extreme provocation.* Alternatively, someone might say, "If she tongue-lashes him very many more times, he may yet blow up," but that does not predict which occasion will be crucial. The eventual choking--or even homicide--may follow a comment that was only a little more cutting than what he had heard so many times before or it may have been nothing new except that this time it followed adverse, stage setting setbacks (no sales made, sharp criticism by a boss, etc.). Violence comes in endless forms, of course, but so often there is an immediate insult or other emotional provocation that initiates the outburst (however insufficient it may seem to others). In any case, given its dependence on a circumstantial trigger, the exact timing and specific nature of a dangerous act can never be predicted.

I also believe that, as in the eruption just discussed, the stage setting and immediate trigger factors are interactive. That is, when one's circumstances have recently been going badly downhill, it takes much less negative input to spark an explosion. As exemplified, a barbed comment that might have been shrugged off or ignored at another time may become "too much to take" at a time of life downturns. An evaluation of these contributions is likely to require interviews of others in the violent individual's life in order to sort out the time frames and sequences; the violent person may poorly perceive them out of an avoidance of the pain of facing the downturns or not wanting to see their connections to his/her behavior.

Overall, the threshold, long-term moderating, and circumstantial factors are all additive and presumably interactive. If, for example, one imagines a relatively young unemployed male whose elevated "489" profile bespeaks cruel indifference and coldness in his childhood as well as a history of gross sexual abuse, who is alcoholic and drunk after being kicked out by a girlfriend, and who then feels insulted by a stranger, then one has all three elements of low threshold for aggression, the young and highly stressed male moderating factors, and the circumstantial setting and trigger to explain his homicidal assault. Thus, in such a case the threshold may be very low with only minimal circumstantial factors, a "walking bomb waiting to be set off." In the case of the police officer above, the threshold was high and the dispositions no more than mixed, but for him the instant provocation was extreme. How much frustration and provocation is it likely to take for a particular individual with his/her own thresholds to commit a violent act in the future is then a matter of complex judgment in which one has to assess the person's psychological makeup, to give weight to a variety of longer-term predictive factors, and to try to anticipate (often an educated guess at best) whether the person is likely to be in seriously provocative circumstances when things are going badly for him/her. A future violent act can never be guaranteed to happen or not to happen, but I do believe the threshold or risk of dangerousness can to a useful degree be predicted.

F6. What about suicide? Can that be predicted?

I believe the same three-phase analysis again applies, that is, there are baseline or threshold risks, longer-term moderating factors, and circumstantial events. As to the threshold, one MMPI pattern marks the greatest risk: this is the combination of having come to believe that one's situation is hopeless (scale 2-D, depression), suffering feelings of worthlessness and self-loathing (scale 8-Sc, schizoid elements), and an unending worry that something still worse is about to happen (scale 7-Pt, obsessiveness). Other patterns also mark very serious even if somewhat less severe risks. One, characterized by feelings of hopelessness (scale 2-D), indifference and emptiness (scale 4-Pd, psychopathy), and a sense of fundamental and loathsome defectiveness (scale 8-Sc) is often associated with risky suicide attempts that coerce interventions and rescue by others. If things go wrong (e.g., phone messages are not picked up in time), an otherwise marginal attempt can prove fatal. Some MMPI patterns are associated with manipulative threats with little apparent rise in the risk that the person will indeed commit suicide. On the other hand, an occasional psychotic patient will startle everyone with a suicide no one saw coming. But these patterns are better conceived as variations of the long-term threshold as distinguished from the immediate or instant suicide risk.

The strongest moderating factors are sex and age. That is, males in or beyond the age range 55 to 65 are clearly the greatest risk (and both sex and age are weighted in the Caldwell Report estimations of baseline suicide risk.). Predictions of adolescent suicides are extremely likely to be wrong, however desperately we may want to predict them, because they occur so rarely out of the entire population of adolescents.

As with violence, one must also consider the circumstantial "stage setting" of a suicide attempt. Were events going downhill for the person (or had been perceived by him/her to be)? Downturns of physical health, losses of financial security, abandonment by loved ones, etc., are hardly mutually exclusive, and all can contribute. Although the MMPI/MMPI-2 can help identify a person's sensitivities, this assessment of stage setting is primarily clinical judgment as to what course the person's life has (or had) been taking, are (or were) there "pressures" toward suicide or circumstances that are (or were) seen to be deteriorating and without escape?

There may well be an immediate precipitant. Consider the circumstances of a chronically depressed male friend whose third marriage had quite recently failed, whose final MMPI was coded "278," who had memorized (word-for-word) a brilliant series of lectures, and who--following a neurologic examination for memory problems--had just been given the diagnosis of an inoperable brain tumor. His only source of gratification was crumbling and soon to be gone. Note the combination of a lowered long-term threshold in an aging single male, his sadly downhill relationship, and the specific suicide-precipitating news.

In summary, I believe the baseline or threshold risk of suicide *is* predictable (e.g., the "278" pattern discussed above, repetitive manic-depressive episodes, and/or intense suicidal ruminations involving a specific, lethal means, etc.). That it will happen on any given day--or necessarily at all--can *never* be predicted with certainty. A clinical judgment that an evident event which was upsetting or crushing to a low threshold or "high-baseline" individual should have led to increased suicide precautions is a legitimate inference. But the long-term risk indicated by the test results and dispositional information must always be evaluated in relation to the person's uncertain future circumstances.

I should reiterate that these formulations of risk evaluation as to violence and suicide are my own formulation of the issues, an attempt that I hope can help sharpen our focus in interviews, reports, and testimony. Although they overlap many elements of professional consensus, this construction is mine an not intended to represent a general agreement in the field.

F7. Can one make a diagnosis with the MMPI/MMPI-2?

No. A diagnosis is the integration of interview information, history data, and whatever tests and measurements are indicated and available. It is a statement about the present status of an individual: what affliction or disorder does this person have? A diagnosis not only identifies a pre-specified syndrome or set of symptoms, but it typically carries implications as to how the person got to be that way (the etiology) along with what treatments are expected to reduce or relieve those symptoms. Thus, making a diagnosis is a clinical, integrative function.

The ethics of the mental health professions are explicit on this point: one does not make a professional diagnosis without an interview (e.g., not by phone, by correspondence, nor by a test alone). This not only protects clients from potential mistakes that face-to-face contact would correct, it also helps to protect the public from charlatans and "con artists." A partial exception would be where the clinician knows the patient well, will diagnose a recurrence of symptoms by phone, and may make a chemical or behavioral prescription. But the face-to-face contact has already been established.

F8. If you can't make a diagnosis from the MMPI/MMPI-2, what good is it?

The MMPI/MMPI-2 is of great value in *differential* diagnosis. How does one decide which of two related diagnoses with overlapping symptoms is the correct one? What is the quality of this person's depression? Might the depression be deceptively severe or easy to overestimate? The function here is to rule in and/or to rule out one or another of the alternative diagnoses. For some MMPI/MMPI-2 patterns--more than others--there are consistencies of etiology, and their presence or absence can be of diagnostic help. There are many consistencies of treatment response by pattern, so this differential discrimination via the MMPI/MMPI-2 affects all of the areas of diagnosis.

Occasional clinicians--especially psychiatrists feeling defensive--will assert that one "cannot make diagnostic statements from the MMPI or MMPI-2, period," e.g., one can only say what the scores are. This is typically a confusion or denial of the above distinction, i.e., the formal *making* of a diagnosis versus the *differentiation* of possible diagnoses (as well as all the other elaborations that can be made from a set of scores). The origin and much of the development of the MMPI/MMPI-2 has been anchored in its clinical correlates, so that there is a solid and extensive justification for making differential diagnostic statements from the inventory.

CASE NOTES:

54

CASE NOTES:

G. WHERE DO COMPUTER-GENERATED REPORTS FIT INTO THE FORENSIC SCHEMA?

G1. Has their use increased?

> Yes: the utilization of--if not for some a considerable dependence on--computer generated narrative reports by mental health experts has increased very substantially in the 1980's and 1990's, and it will likely continue into the foreseeable future. There are many tradeoffs in this, both major advantages and potentially serious problems.

G2. What are the advantages spurring this increase?

> One advantage is economic. It is possible to obtain computer generated interpretations very quickly and inexpensively for the amount of information received. Many clinicians feel their time is better spent seeing clients and assembling individual reports than in researching MMPI manuals for interpretive information: let the MMPI/MMPI-2 experts do that.
>
> A related advantage is the quantity of information. A computer can score as many scales as one wants in milliseconds, and it can immediately print out a variety of summaries, indexes, lists of interview-noteworthy items (the so-called "Critical Items"), etc. In contrast, it takes close to a half-hour just to score the basic scales and plot them on a profile sheet by hand. A secretary would be tied up for one or even several hours to produce as much as a computer can print out in seconds.
>
> A third advantage is objectivity. Jury members may be impressed by testimony that every sentence in the computer report was written well before the person even took the test. That is, they can trust that the choice of words in the report was in no way influenced by anyone's bias in the case at

issue. Even if there is a slightly negative overall bias in that the MMPI/MMPI-2 computer-generated reports were often written with relevance for psychotherapy in mind, this "looking for relevant pathology" orientation applies equally to all people taking the test and cannot be selective with respect to the immediate participants.

G3. Is there any theoretical justification for trusting computer-generated reports?

There is a theoretical underpinning for this procedure that is often forgotten or ignored by clinicians (if even understood and appreciated). This is the work initiated by Dr. Paul Meehl of the University of Minnesota (1954) on the issue of "clinical versus statistical prediction." By statistical or "actuarial" prediction he meant that a person's behaviors would be predicted in a broadly mechanical sense, i.e., by objective formulas from tests such as the MMPI or any of a wide variety of sources of objective information about the person (past school grades, IQ scores, medical history items, lab findings, etc.). An actuary retained by a life or automobile insurance company is doing the same sort of thing, which is to base insurance rates on the likelihood of particular outcomes (injuries and deaths, auto repair costs, etc.) as a function of objective data such as age, sex, driver training, past driving record, being in the military, etc. By clinical prediction Dr. Meehl meant the ordinary clinical activity of studying an array of information and subjectively predicting the *same* outcome. He predicted that the accuracy of actuarial prediction would consistently equal or exceed that of clinical prediction. This proposition has turned out to have what is in the social and medical sciences an astounding, effectively 100% validation since he first proposed it in 1954. Many clinicians, whose careers and professional identities are planted in their abilities to make predictions from interviews (especially psychiatrists), are threatened by this data; they strongly tend to ignore it if they know of it. But it remains overwhelmingly true that, if one has a validated prediction formula, when one goes against it one is, on the average, sure to lose accuracy. One might be right in an individual case that the formula would have missed, but over a series of cases, individual judgment has *never* gained ground.

The narrative reports generated by Caldwell Report are actuarial in the sense that the interpretive material is case-based. The content of the sentences comes from thousands of cases seen over many years and the consistencies of behavior that have emerged within each of the "code types" as discussed above. There is also a large literature on the meanings of different patterns on the MMPI that is integrated into the interpretations. Even the sentences are probabilistic in wording, e.g., "many . . .," "some . . .," or only "a few similar cases have shown . . .," and other comparable wordings are intentional gradations of probability. A key advantage of this procedure is that such a system can recall the unusual and idiosyncratic characteristics of rarely occurring test patterns. These have been shown to be the ones on which clinicians most often go wrong. The computer system may rarely make that prediction, but its memory is indefinite in size and over time, so that when the very unusual case comes up, if it has been seen before and recorded, it will be remembered and interpreted.

G4. Are there problems with this approach?

(1) One objection is that a computer-generated report cannot allow for a person's history, e.g., for rare or unique events, specific traumas, immediate circumstances, etc., that could be influencing a person's test responses or current behavior. Obviously, the enormous range of things that can occur to an individual are beyond entering into the rules or algorithms by which a computer program operates (on the practical basis of time and program size, not necessarily hypothetically). Clinicians have a tendency to overweight such rarities, and

this is a place where they are particularly vulnerable to going wrong by overemphasizing their importance. The actuarial formula is not so much swayed or affected by a unique item even if it does directly or indirectly allow for it, and hence it goes wrong less often.

This computer-report "failure" to allow for the person's history is a mis-assignment of responsibilities. The computer-generated report or "actuarial function" is a delineation of what is *typical* or *characteristic* of a person with the same or a sufficiently similar pattern of scores. Determining *how* the person came to that psychological state and set of attitudes is the "clinical function." Although the test results may give us strong clues as to whether the person's current state is likely to be stable or transitory, it is a clinical or case-based judgment as to how the person got that way as well as just what will likely alter--or not alter--that pattern in the near or more distant future. The responsibility of the "actuarial interpretation" of the MMPI/MMPI-2 is to best reflect the person's pattern of behaviors and emotions. The responsibility of the clinician is to integrate that information with the interview, history, and whatever other information is available to him/her.

(2) A related objection is the question as to the inability of computer-generated reports to account for special circumstances of testing. Again, a thorough analysis of the person's test taking attitude (I believe this to be more detailed and specific in the Caldwell Report printouts than any other source) needs to be integrated by the clinician with the latter's personal knowledge of any unusual or irregular circumstances of testing. That is, it is the clinician's judgment as to what part of any distortion in the person's responding is to be attributed to any special circumstances or irregularity in the test administration and testing situation.

(3) An opposite problem (one that surprised me when it first

began to occur) is that of categorical trust in the computer report. This was as if some clinicians were so impressed with the accuracy of the reports that they felt everything had to be true. The "flip side" of this was that, once a specific prediction was clearly wrong, then the whole report had to be distrusted or rejected. Psychologists are much more extensively trained in considering their interpretations of their data to be probabilistic than are psychiatrists and social workers. The latter are prone to expect that a category, e.g., a diagnosis, will be either true or false, so that treating the various propositions in a computer-generated report as having varying degrees of likelihood or applicability is uncomfortable if not alien to such categorical, "all-or-nothing" thinking.

A related concern to psychologists is what they see as the abuse of computer-generated interpretations by psychiatrists. A psychiatrist with little or no formal training in quantitative personality measurement or the application of personality tests may go into court treating a computer report as if it were "the word of god," at least as long as it supports his/her position. This may operate to the exclusion of different tests and other data that might be qualifying or even contradictory as well as excluding the use by the court of the testimony of psychologists who might be expected to present more balanced and accurate interpretations of the MMPI/MMPI-2 and other test data. There have been objections by psychologists that Caldwell Report and other computerized test-interpretation services should not provide computer-generated reports to non-psychologist professionals lest they be too literally or selectively relied on or otherwise abused. I believe this to be an over-reaction, that the problem is one of educating the forensic community rather than prohibiting psychiatrists direct access to such reports.

(4) The question can be asked, are such computerized systems not put together by humans and therefore subject to errors of

judgment and other biases? Such interpretive programs are called "expert systems" in the literature, reflecting the fact that they are in part dependent on the expertise of the person(s) who write them. A distinction can be made, however, between the accumulation of essentially actuarial information or content that has been established as specific to an MMPI/MMPI-2 pattern versus the weights or score-cutoffs that determine when a sentence will be entered. The latter, e.g., including how strong the intensity of an entry should be ("severely depressed" rather than "moderately to severely depressed," etc.), is a particularly judgmental decision that would rarely be drawn exactly the same even by two experts on the MMPI/MMPI-2. Hence the title, "an expert system." There are in general two aspects to the evaluation of such an expert system: one is the accuracy with which the output reflects case knowledge and the established research, and the second is the consensus of other experts as to the quality of development in the writing of the algorithms. An independent source would be the Eighth Mental Measurement Yearbook (Buros).

As can be seen, the function of the actuary (e.g., myself) and the function of the clinician can be easily differentiated. The actuarial responsibility is to provide the most accurate, specific, and usable information available as to what is typical and characteristic of a person "who answered as did this person." The clinician's function is to integrate this data with the idiosyncrasies of the individual case as well as the specific issues raised and the questions about which the court needs information. If properly understood, these functions are complementary and not at odds.

G5. How are the actuarial test results by themselves best understood in the context of writing a forensic psychological report?

For purposes of reaching a clinical opinion about an individual, actuarial test results are best viewed as hypotheses. Before reaching a firm conclusion about any individual based on the test results, it is important to confirm or disconfirm the test predictions with real world data about the litigant in question. If the key features of the test-based predictions are generally confirmed by such known, real-world data about the person, then one can be much more confident that the remainder of the predictions generated by the test are likely to be accurate.

An accurate but cautious overall introduction to the use of computer-generated test results in a forensic evaluation report might read like the following:

> *Results of Psychological Testing.* Personality test results reflect characteristics of persons who have provided test response patterns that are similar to those of (this current individual). The computer-generated interpretations presented in this report are hypotheses to be integrated with other available information. They reflect expert analyses and predictions of behavior based on what is typical for subjects with similar test results. Although the results are presented in an affirmative manner, they are probabilistic in nature and need to be confirmed or disconfirmed by other data; both the clinician and the reader of this report should be conscious of the weight given to any one specific statement. The extent to which these personality patterns and deficits pre-existed the legal events in question or are the sequelae of those events is a matter of clinical judgment and cannot

be inferred from the test results alone. Such an inference is a clinical opinion as to the relative contributions of the person's longstanding tendencies and the effects of more recent events.

G6. How might the use of actuarial information be relevant in the direct examination of an expert witness?

A dialogue with the expert witness could take the following form:

(Direct examining attorney, "DEA") Doctor, you made use of Dr. Caldwell's report in reaching your conclusions. You referred to Dr. Caldwell's report as "actuarial." What did you mean by that?

(Expert Witness, "EW") Let me explain. We are most familiar with the word "actuarial" in such circumstances as automobile insurance rates (however we feel about them!). The insurance company hires people, their actuaries, to calculate probable outcomes by various available indicators such as the person's age and sex, whether the person has had a driver training course, the person's previous driving record, etc. The company rates are adjusted according to this actuarial information.

As to the MMPI, there is extensive research as to what scores and what patterns of scores are associated with what kinds of behaviors, for example, with what symptoms, what diagnoses, what future risks or dangers, and so forth. Dr. Caldwell's report provided me with very detailed information as to how a person with (Mr./Ms. X's) scores would likely respond to (his/her) life circumstances. Given his detailed, expert knowledge of the MMPI, Dr. Caldwell is in this way functioning as my actuary.

(DEA) Is there any reason for a clinical psychologist such as yourself not just to look at the scores and interpret them?

(EW) There is a large number of studies showing, not only with the MMPI but in predicting medical diagnoses, school success, parole violation, and many other outcomes, that actuarial prediction is *always* at least as accurate and usually *more* accurate than what we might call "eyeball judgment."

(DEA) Why would that be?

(EW) What we would call the actuarial formula gives the available information the best or optimal weights. The individual, even if personally unbiased, is prone to error because he or she will give too much weight to some facts and too little weight to other items.

(DEA) So, even if not biased, the individual can easily go wrong?

(EW) Yes, even in a neutral situation.

(DEA) But in a trial?

(EW) In an adversarial situation such as in court, even if one is trying hard to be objective, it is very easy to quite sincerely over-weigh and under-weigh different data according to how they fit your expectations and desires to support the side you have taken.

(DEA) And if the clinical examiner *is* biased?

(EW) Then it is very easy to take a few bits and

pieces of information and go far off with them. [Here or subsequently a grossly biased opinion for the other side could be contrasted to the objective information from the MMPI/MMPI-2 actuarial report.]

(DEA) So you use Dr. Caldwell's report in part to correct for bias because it is in no way influenced by the facts in this case?

(EW) Exactly. I would like to point out that every sentence, every word, in Dr. Caldwell's report was written *before* (Mr./Ms. X) was asked to take the MMPI-2. His report was in no way whatsoever influenced by any knowledge of (Mr./Ms. X). It is an entirely objective, actuarial report based solely on (Mr./Ms. X's) *own* responses to the items on the test.

To the extent that the MMPI/MMPI-2 results reflected in a Caldwell Report are material to the matter at issue, a dialogue such as the above could help to establish their objectivity to the court. In certain circumstances, particularly child custody and job screening contexts where relatively normal profiles are typical, it would be accurate to note that the Caldwell Report narrative material was written with an overall focus on psychotherapy or treatment intake, that is, what are the issues about which a psychotherapist would want to be informed? This does constitute a slight selective bias in that the reports then search for information that would be important for a treating clinician to be aware of (more than strengths and assets), so that primarily within the "normal range" (see section F3) there is a "negative" bias in this search for problem areas. This tilt applies, of course, to all profiles and all interpretations, and it therefore is in no way differentially biased for or against any individual person or case.

CASE NOTES:

CASE NOTES:

H. PARENTING AND THE MMPI/MMPI-2

The following section is specifically oriented toward the use of the MMPI/MMPI-2 in child custody cases. It is somewhat more MMPI-technical at some points than the preceding, but the intent is to discuss the MMPI/MMPI-2 issues that repeatedly do come up in these cases.

H1. Is there specific research on parenting?

> There is less formal research in the professional literature on parenting in association with individual MMPI patterns than one would expect. Perhaps the most relevant data we have has come from the MMPI profiles of mothers and fathers of children seen in child guidance clinics and related child and adolescent treatment settings (e.g., Hafner, A. J., Butcher, J. N., Hall, M. D., & Quast, W., 1969). There are some general hierarchies that have been established, although the data are general and not always consistent. For example, the profiles of parents in such settings are *on the average* (1) more disturbed than the profiles of "normal" or "control" samples, e.g., P.T.A. members, but they are (2) less disturbed than the profiles of adult patients seeking individual psychotherapy. One can show that parents of schizophrenic children tend to be somewhat more disturbed (with surprisingly little consistency as to type of disturbance) than is true for parents of children with serious medical disabilities, but in a few studies with data on the point, the parents of schizophrenic children were less disturbed than those of "acting out" or conduct disordered children. Some studies suggested that the greater the differences between the profiles of the two parents, the greater the disturbances of the children (e.g., inconsistent attitudes and discipline), but other data fail to support this finding. Children of parents who have been divorced tend to show more aggressive behavior and acting out than children of parents who have been continuously married.

Among the MMPI/MMPI-2 scales discussed elsewhere (see sections A6, H3, and H4), there is a tendency for scales 3-Hy (Conversion Hysteria), 4-Pd (Psychopathic Deviate), and 6-Pa (Paranoia) to be the most consistently elevated among children seen in these treatment settings (whatever the marital status of the parents). This is relevant in that these are the same three scales most commonly seen in parents litigating over custody. It has often been my experience to feel quite uncomfortable with the profiles of *both* custody litigating parents, that neither looks like a "good parent" and sometimes--despite their protestations--neither looks like the sort of person who really *wants* to be a parent or to spend major amounts of time at parenting activities. So often they seem caught in old battles that cannot be forgiven and forgotten, battles that are so immediately and painfully destructive to the children.

Looking at MMPI/MMPI-2 profiles of adults in relation to intrafamilial traumas in childhood is also relevant. Adult psychotherapy patients with 3-Hy/4-Pd patterns often had to be over-controlled and to tell "white lies" as children to escape punishment such as explosive paternal outbursts. There has recently (late 1980's, 1990's) been a large increase in the readiness of mental health clinicians to ask about sexual abuse (greater professional concern about the issue and wanting not to be embarrassed for having failed to inquire). A single pattern on the MMPI (defined by the primary elevations on scales 4-Pd and 8-Sc) has emerged as more characteristic than any other in the victims of sexual abuse. Having these two scales highest does not, of course, guarantee a history of sexual abuse, but where there is sexual abuse in the history, these two scales are often relatively elevated and not infrequently the two most elevated scales. Several psychotic patterns are commonly associated with histories of physical abuse, and parental abusers often have somewhat similar patterns. Men in prison convicted of sexual offenses are relatively heterogeneous in their profiles, although they are often most elevated on scale 4-Pd and come from families marked by unwantedness and indifference toward them as children. Again, these are essentially averaged data or reflect recurring tendencies, and strong one-to-one relations between parenting and child outcomes have not been directly established on a research basis.

In general, the major problem in this obvious deficit of substantially parenting-specific research is that there are so many different parent personalities and complex interactions between them. For example, how does one separate what in the parent's psychopathology contributed to the development of problematic behavior in the child versus what part of the parent's distress and disturbance may have been in response to the child's disorder? How does one determine what in the child was due to the pathology of one parent (and not the other) vs. the interaction of differences between the parents? Is an MMPI/ MMPI-2 profile obtained at one point in time an accurate measure of the person's parenting attitudes over many past and future years, or has it been significantly altered by current frustrations and stresses in the person's life, particularly the stress of litigation? Children in many families have strong needs to differentiate themselves from their siblings so that one-to-one relations between parent pathology and child pathology often emerge as inconsistent. Beyond all this, recent research has attributed much more weight to genetic influences on personality than has previously been appreciated or integrated into psychological conceptualizations. In summary, one would have to have MMPI/MMPI-2 and behavioral data on thousands of families as well as great amounts of data on the development of psychopathology in the children to begin to sort out all these particular relationships.

H2. Is clinical experience with the MMPI/MMPI-2 nevertheless relevant and helpful?

This is clearly of major and sometimes crucial weight in child custody evaluations and testimony. When so many variations of personality as well as complex circumstances are relevant to one's recommendations, there is no choice but to accept integrative human judgment as the basis for our decisions. Consistent with the above, clinicians working with these cases do see numerous consistencies in the particular MMPI/MMPI-2 patterns that recur. Indeed, specific MMPI patterns have been shown to predict the same behavioral tendencies in very different settings and circumstances of assessment. These patterns are then foundational to the opinion of the professional expert.

H3. What are the spousal role implications of the three most common MMPI custody conflict patterns?

The MMPI 34/43 code[1] (scales 3-Hy and 4-Pd higher than any other of the eight "clinical scales") is marked by a "role consciousness" that others often see as role-playing if not at times as phony or misleading. There is a tendency to romanticize the partner when falling in love so that the human shortcomings that emerge later are like "a different person from the one I married." Upward status mobility is relatively common with a strong sensitivity to insults to one's social

---

The emphasis here is on the MMPI (as compared to the MMPI-2) code. The scores generating normal range MMPI profiles in which scale 4-Pd is highest or second highest are very likely to produce different codes on the MMPI-2. Although a potentially technical and obscure point in testimony, a set of such scores plotted *only* on the norms for the MMPI-2 is very vulnerable to misinterpretation and an underestimation of the individual's problems and contributions to family difficulties. Ignoring the behavioral implications of the corresponding MMPI pattern (and the specificity of the 50 years of research on it) would be hard to defend.

image and pride. Frustrations are expressed indirectly; resentments that the other person "has failed to measure up" may be saved up until they come out in explosive outbursts, the intensity and consequences on others being subsequently denied. Personal problems in general are rigidly denied, so that criticisms are apt to be seen as needlessly unkind and hostile attacks.

The MMPI 36/63 code (with scales 3-Hy and 6-Pa highest in either order), probably the second most common, is similar in the denial of personal problems along with the status aspirations and sensitivities, but it is particularly marked by control needs and more fixed judgments of virtues and deficiencies in others. Personal attractiveness and needs to be found attractive are emphasized in association with both of these patterns. A related and perhaps third most frequent pattern is the 46/64 pattern, defined by scales 4-Pd and 6-Pa highest. Here there typically are problems of pride, willfulness, unreleased resentments, and jealousy with a potential for issues of temper control and controlling others with the threat of losing control of one's temper.

All three of these code types are characterized by an inability to forgive and forget. The insults to the person's public role, the needless hurts, and the violations of marital obligations must be atoned or somehow compensated for. But emotionally they can never be. These people remain "trapped in the past" for long periods of time, even well into subsequent remarriages. These expressions of this inability to forgive and forget are then typically very damaging to the children.

When one or both of the scales in each of these pairs is well within the normal range, e.g., below a T-score of 65 on the MMPI or below T-60 on the MMPI-2 with 4-Pd close to T-55 or lower, then the above tendencies are usually mild and not impairing (assuming a not excessively defensive set of responses). If one or more of these three scales are T-70 or higher on the MMPI or T-65 or above on the MMPI-2, despite the pressure of the circumstances to look healthy and normal, there are likely to be serious and chronic problems in both spousal relationships and parenting. Intermediate scores then reflect repetitive problems that are, however, usually seen as "not out of control."

H4. What are the parenting implications of these three common patterns (i.e., 34/43, 36/63, and 46/64)?

As can be anticipated from what has been discussed, none are good patterns for parenting (particularly with increasing elevations on scale 4-Pd in the 34/43 and 46/64 codes). When scale 4 is elevated, they tend to be egocentric, and attention to the child or children is typically uneven and undependable over time. It is apt to vary from dramatic showings of attention and favor to moments of coldness to the child's wants or even to occasions of failure to respond to the child's urgent distress. The fairly common normal range elevation on scale 6-Pa is problematic in the rigidity or fixity of judgments, especially when the code is 36/63. This may entail both over-identifying alliances with the child and severity when the child fails to comply with high parental standards and expectations. As discussed above, the 34/43 code has particularly and often been found in parents of children seen in child treatment settings. The 34/43 mother may protest to the professional that she has done all the right things for the child and cannot understand his/her misconduct: "I've taken him/her to all the lessons and doctors. I've done everything a mother can, and it hasn't worked; it's up to you to fix this child." A central problem, of course, is the lack of spontaneous warmth and affection (e.g., rarely well provided in the middle of a bridge game) and the associated tendency of the child to act out or to become aggressive in the absence of loving attention.

The single scale that is most consistently adverse to parenting appears to be scale 4-Pd (with due and extensive qualifications as to the adversity of elevations on *any* of the eight clinical scales). A central issue here is of deficient bonding. Typically, the parent with scale 4-Pd elevated was not warmly and lovingly bonded to his/her own parents (whether they were indifferent, abusive, professionally preoccupied, or otherwise "not there"). This limitation or shallowness of emotional attachment is apt to be recapitulated with that person's own child or children. An unwanted and unbonded child is then a candidate for difficulties in developing an integrated and socialized conscience as well as in the subsequent establishment of stable adult relationships. It should be noted that preliminary twin research data suggest a strongly genetic component to scale 4-Pd, whatever processes underlie the development of elevations on this scale. A long-term history of egocentrically aggressive behavior by a parent with a higher elevation on this scale (even if still within the "normal range") could be interpreted as consistent with the transmission of a genetic vulnerability as well as cause for concern as to the perpetuation of deficient bonding.

H5. What can be said about alienation of affection?

Problems of alienation of affection are most often seen in association with elevations on scale 6-Pa. One aspect of this scale is a repetitive tendency to perceive and categorize others as "for me or against me." (Only toward the psychotic extreme is almost everyone seen as being "against me.") Undue attention is then paid to whether the children are "allied with the 'ex' or with me." This sensitivity may lead the parent (with scale 6-Pa elevated) to be the first to raise the question as to the *other* parent's alienation of the child's (or children's) affections, often with such a narrow focus on the child's responses about or to the other parent as not to see any personal contribution to the problem. To be under repeated, polarizing pressures to align with one parent against the other is a particularly destructive milieu for children. This can be quite difficult to defuse, although our primary responsibility to the children urges that we do all we can; to avoid arrangements that could promote or intensify alienation of affection whenever we reasonably can is probably of merciful benefit to the child, although the cruel destructiveness may need to be confronted straightforwardly if an alienating pattern has become established.

H6. What can be determined about child sexual abuse?

Each parent's word against the other is, of course, a most difficult problem, the unresolvable "he said, she said" dialogue. The MMPI/MMPI-2 offers less evidence or certainty as to the presence or absence of sexual abuse than might be expected. Expressions of sexual behavior are highly idiosyncratic, and there are very few consistent associations of MMPI patterns to each of the extraordinary range and diversity of specific human predilections and perversions. Two exceptions are that, when elevated, (1) the combination of scales 4-Pd and 8-Sc (the 48/84 code) commented on earlier has a substantial association with sexual abuse and perversion including emotionally tormenting or even physically sadomasochistic behavior, and (2) the combination of scales 4-Pd and 9-Ma (the 49/94 code) is associated with a marked accentuation of sexual activity of whatever sort. Particularly troublesome in custody cases is an unverifiable accusation of sexual abuse against a parent with a 34/43 (3-Hy/4-Pd) code. Already denying any personal contribution to the child's problems, an accusation of abuse is apt to be denied vehemently whether true or false. As already touched on, the one consistency is that when scale 4-Pd is elevated (especially over T-70 MMPI or over T-65 MMPI-2), there is a strong potential for atypical or deviant sexual activity (the Pd scale is the highest or second highest scale for about 60%

of men *in prison* for sexual offenses; Erickson, Luxenberg, Walbek, & Seely, 1987). It is critical to keep in mind, however, that all of this is group data and individual expression can vary greatly from one person to the next. Indeed, a "normal range" elevation on scale 4-Pd would be only *weak evidence against* deviant sexuality, and if 4-Pd were highest or second in the code and also T-64 or more (MMPI) or over T-55 (MMPI-2), sexual abuse would clearly not be ruled out. A complete absence of elevation on this scale (e.g., a T-score at or under 55 on the MMPI norms, about T-45 or lower on the MMPI-2 norms) would be stronger (but by no means conclusive) evidence *against* the likelihood of sexual abusiveness or perversion. In general, the MMPI/MMPI-2 can be only one part of the data arguing for or against an allegation of child sexual abuse.

CASE NOTES:

CASE NOTES:

I. REPORTS AND TESTIMONY

I1. When do custody experts get in trouble?

A recurrent and at times awkward problem is that an inexperienced (or at times even a more experienced) evaluator will see one spouse, be attentive and sympathetic, take in that spouse's point of view, and then see the other spouse through the eyes of the first. Although the interpretation of the MMPI/MMPI-2 has a natural objectivity to it, there is clinical judgment in applying it to the individual person's behavior and circumstances. Here there can be a bias of interpretation in which selective, adverse aspects of the pattern are mentally fitted to pre-existing negative expectations of the second party. If such a "first client bias" were evident, the evaluator might be asked (1) what statements he/she made to the *first* person being evaluated regarding the fact that the *other* party (e.g., ex-spouse) will also be seen, (2) was he/she explicit that both stories will be considered, (3) did he/she stress that his/her primary responsibility is to the children, (4) did he/she remind the client that the evaluator's responsibility is to put the whole picture together as best as can be done, etc. This first-client bias seems to come up most often when a psychotherapist, trained in and oriented toward sympathetic understanding, first begins to do custody evaluations. Such assertions (of giving equal consideration to the opposite party) get left out because they are uncomfortable if not alien to the therapist's empathetic approach. In contrast to the therapeutic role, of course, the custody evaluator needs to be in part a questioning detective, exploring contradictory assertions and balancing one person's story against another's, and he/she needs to protect his/her independence of judgment with skill and care.

I have testified as a witness or rebuttal witness to restore balance in just such cases. I have observed an unexpected frequency of elevations on scale 6-Pa (reflecting subtler, normal range paranoid trends) in the patterns of the first-seen spouses in these cases. A few have obtained the specific pattern combining scales 6-Pa and 9-Ma, the 69/96 code type, which characterizes a person who is highly vigilant as to who is for or against his/her interests and security, a person who is strongly energetic and at times intimidating in order to protect those interests. In these instances the tendency to line people up either "for me or against me" associated with scale 6-Pa appeared to have been operating in the initial interview setting.

A related and sometimes subtle but potentially problematic issue is the natural human tendency to take a liking to one person more than another. The relatively more common litigant codes discussed above, especially 3-Hy/4-Pd and 4-Pd/6-Pa (along with 4-Pd/9-Ma which latter is of secondary frequency in custody cases but still a relatively common pattern), identify people who are initially appealing and potentially describable as "seductive." Such a like/dislike bias could become noticeable in terms of a selectivity of data that is cited and points of evidence that are emphasized. This is, however, both awkward to allege and hard to prove, so it becomes a matter of establishing a preponderance of evidence of selectivity, but it may need to be listened for and--if apparent and probative--pointed out.

I2. Can hypothetical questions become a problem?

Yes: I would specifically urge that the wording of more complex hypothetical questions be rehearsed carefully. I have been asked such questions where I could agree with all of the many elements except to the wording of a single one, which made a simple "yes" impossible (to the direct examining attorney's chagrin). Edit any hypothetical question phrase by phrase before it is asked and not on the stand. An attorney's familiarity with this present document might well facilitate the formulation of such hypothetical questions.

I3. What about test-item by test-item cross examination?

> It is, of course, the attorney's privilege to examine the expert witness using the MMPI/MMPI-2 on an item-by-item basis. This is often disconcerting to the expert who interprets the profile (and the other tests as well) in terms of scores and patterns rather than individual items. Indeed, the single item responses are often "news" to the expert who has not even examined them at that level. The more or less reflexive--and honest--response is that it is the scores and the pattern of scores that are predictive of the person's attitudes and behaviors. Although one could reiterate this response in a "broken record" fashion, it quickly feels like an unsatisfying dodge to the judge and jury (it does help if this "pattern of scores rather than single-item interpretation" has been anticipated on direct and one can refer back those earlier comments). Another response is to remind the jury that the MMPI/MMPI-2 items were intentionally written to be ambiguous in order to tap a wide variety of attitudes; whereas we each have our own presumption as to what an item means, the next person's presumption can be quite different.

> Items cited in the text of the report can be made (on cross examination) to sound as if more gravely warning than the evaluator took them to be, e.g., having been in trouble over one's sex behavior, having been in trouble with the law, having used alcohol excessively, or other selected Critical Items. There are several possible responses to this, although it can be difficult not to sound defensive. Firstly, items cited within the Caldwell Report text as well as on the Critical Items listing are *interview prompts*: an item is "critical" for interview purposes if it *may* lead to important, specific information (being plotted against, hearing voices, etc.). Such responses should be followed up during the evaluation since it is potentially discrediting to have to say no if asked, "Did you inquire about his/her response to this item on *your* list, Doctor?" Secondly, profile data may well contradict the cross

examiner's implications. For example, someone with a relatively low score on the MacAndrew Alcoholism Scale (Mac) may nevertheless say true to having used alcohol excessively. Inquiry in the interview may well reflect a response based on a pattern of intermittent or even very infrequent alcohol use that is not at all the daily dependence that is frequently associated with high scores on the Mac scale. (One client had been deeply embarrassed at having fallen off a horse coming home drunk from a party as an adolescent, and because of this he had never let himself get close to being drunk in all his adult life; on this basis he said "true," he had used alcohol excessively.) "Trouble with the law" may be no more than the present dispute (and the "chronic lawbreaker" implications contradicted by a lower score on scale 4-Pd), and sexual trouble may be no more than an adolescent embarrassment or an unhappy abortion many years past--or something that would be much more trivial still to most people. The citing of an item for interview checking may need to be explicitly distinguished from the behavioral predictions of the remainder of the report, again much more easily done on direct than cross examination.

At times items can be pointed out as not what they seem. As a personal example, a psychotic murder defendant had a high score (five of the six possible items) on the Ma1 (Opportunism or Amorality) subscale. The district attorney had found them, made sure I had an answer sheet, and then read the items to the court asking me what the defendant's response was to each (e.g., not blaming a person for grabbing everything he can get in this world, hoping an entertainingly clever crook would get by with it, always being disgusted with the law if a criminal is freed through the arguments of a smart lawyer (false), etc.). My response was that, although the items did sound sociopathic, only one of the six is actually on the psychopathic or Pd scale. In contrast, they are manic items that reflect an urgency or desperation that one has to take advantage of situations in order to survive. I reiterated--

on redirect--that taking items out of context easily creates a false impression as to their meaning. Although I would not say this erased the questions presumably raised in the jurors' minds, I believe it did to some degree reduce or neutralize them.

For the MMPI-pattern-sophisticated psychologist, such item-by-item questioning is often, as noted, an annoying digression. Basically, one searches for ways to return to the basic point that it is the scores and the patterns among the scores that give us the important information as to what to expect of an individual. One can stress that, (1) because one would have to ask the person what each and every item meant to him/her, as well as considering (2) their unexpected contributions to different scales and (3) their changeability over time (items get changed much more than the scores change), *single items cannot be independently interpreted.* For example, the expert might respond, "A major advantage of giving him/her a test with 567 items is that it will cover far more topics than I can take the time to ask him/her about one by one. Of course I did not ask him/her about every single item. I want to know where the items 'piled up,' that is, *which types of items he/she responded to the most.* That is what tells us what to expect of him/her."

14. What if I am faced with an opinion that I believe does not fit the individual(s) or their test data?

A first issue to check is test validity as discussed under Test-Taking Attitude in section B above. The two conscious distortion scales discussed, Malingering Positive (Mp) and Social Desirability (Sd, by Wiggins) are potentially of direct relevance. If they are elevated, the narrative analysis by Caldwell Report will discuss these in detail, and this can be of assistance in arguments such as that an opposite party (in such contexts as child custody, job application appeals, restoration to active police duty, etc.) was deceiving or hiding problem areas on the test (versus the equivocal nature of a high K score in a higher socioeconomic status individual, as previously discussed in section B). Where there may be a motive to exaggerate or malinger, the differentiation of atypical responding (also discussed above) can be broken down as to intentional overstatement (the Ds or Dissimulation scale elevated), valid and severe disturbance (considerable F without much Ds), or unsophisticated lower S.E.S. responding (very low Ss scale).

If the defensive/self-critical biasing of responses does not answer the misfit to the case, then consultation with an MMPI-knowledgeable clinical psychologist is indicated. Here the issue is whether the professional opinion accurately represents common thinking as to the meaning of the MMPI/MMPI-2 profile(s) at issue or represents a selective, biased, incomplete, or otherwise distorted interpretation of the data. A Caldwell Report or other actuarial source, as discussed in section G., can strongly support the exposure of a mistaken of misleading interpretation of the test.

If a person with a valid, elevated profile, e.g., one or especially two or more of the eight clinical scales significantly elevated (at or over T 70, MMPI, or at or over T 65, MMPI-2) is dismissed as an "Adjustment Disorder" with a clear implication of no serious or even significant psychopathology, then this could be straightforwardly presented as a biased underestimation of the person's emotional difficulties; the profile is definitely in the "abnormal range." Conversely, a representation of serious or impairing psychopathology in someone with an unelevated or "normal range" profile would have to be defended strongly as to defensive covering over or whatever other explanation as to why such purported pathology did not show up on the MMPI/MMPI-2. More technical issues as to bias with respect to the precise meaning of the code type would, of course, need psychological expertise as to the interpretation of patterns on the MMPI/MMPI-2.

CASE NOTES:

CASE NOTES:

Psychological References

American Psychological Association (1992). Ethical of Principles of Psychologists and Code of Conduct. American Psychologist: 47, 1597-1611.

Archer, R. (1992). MMPI-A: Assessing adolescent psychopathology. Hillsdale, NJ: Lawrence Erlbaum Associates. (The resource book on the MMPI-A.)

Buros, O. K. (Ed.). (1978). The eighth mental measurements yearbook. Highland Park, NJ: Gryphon Press. (Contains comparisons of various computer interpretation systems then in use.)

Butcher, J. N., Dahlstrom, W. G., Graham, J. R., Tellegen, A., & Kaemmer, B. (1989). Minnesota Multiphasic Personality Inventory (MMPI-2). Manual for administration and scoring. Minneapolis: University of Minnesota Press. (This is the manual for the MMPI-2 detailing the changes made in the revision, who can give the MMPI-2, many tables and item listings.)

Butcher, J. N., Graham, J. R., Williams, C. L., & Ben-Porath, Y. S. (1990). Development and use of the MMPI-2 content scales. Minneapolis, MN: University of Minnesota Press. (Basic development plus a few interpretive thoughts on a series of "content scales" that reflect the relative frequencies of responses to MMPI-2 items about specific topics; see review by Caldwell, A. B. [1991], Contemporary Psychology, 36, 560-561.)

Caldwell, A. B. (1988). The MMPI supplemental scale manual. Los Angeles, CA: Caldwell Report. (This summarizes the subscales and supplemental/research scales scored by Caldwell Report including scales Ds, Mp, Sd, and Ss; it was written with a practical clinical-use orientation.)

Caldwell, A. B. (1990, August). Measurement of the human condition. Paper presented at the meeting of the American Psychological Association, Boston, Ma. (Summary of comparisons of the MMPI vs. the MMPI-2.)

Caldwell, A. B. (1996). MMPI AND MMPI-2: Scales, theory, and interpretation. (Cassette Recordings). Los Angeles: Caldwell Report. (The first of ten audiotaped workshop sessions covers a detailed comparison of the MMPI vs. the MMPI-2, including the arguments for plotting the MMPI-2 profile on the MMPI norms.)

Caldwell, A. B. (1997). Whither Goest our Redoubtable Mentor, the MMPI/MMPI-2? Journal of Personality Assessment, 68, 47-68. (Includes a more detailed theoretical discussion of MMPI vs. MMPI-2 and a review of the practical importance of measuring socioeconomic status.)

Dahlstrom, W. G., & Dahlstrom, L. E. (1980). Basic Readings on the MMPI: A new selection on personality measurement. Minneapolis, MN: University of Minnesota Press. (The original articles on the development of the 13 basic scales plus carefully chosen summaries of other scales. Five articles cover various applications of the MMPI including a discussion of asking private questions or not and an appellate court ruling on personnel screening with the MMPI.)

Dahlstrom, W. G., Lachar, D., & Dahlstrom, L. E. (1986). MMPI patterns of American minorities. Minneapolis, MN: University of Minnesota Press. (The definitive book on black-white research, demonstrating that the MMPI differences observed are essentially associated with socioeconomic variables and are not due to any consistent racial differences.)

Dahlstrom, W. G., Welsh, G. S., & Dahlstrom, L. E. (1972). An

MMPI handbook: Vol. I. Clinical interpretation. Minneapolis, MN: University of Minnesota Press. (Exceptionally thorough coverage of the research on the scales, the two point codes, and basic MMPI information including comparisons of several computer-generated interpretation systems.)

Dahlstrom, W. G., Welsh, G. S., & Dahlstrom, L. E. (1975). An MMPI handbook: Vol. II. Research applications. Minneapolis, MN: University of Minnesota Press. (A remarkably comprehensive summary with a listing of about 6000 research studies and 455 scales. This is the prime reference for research--up to 1975--in essentially all the areas in which the MMPI has been applied.)

Erickson, W. D., Luxenberg, M. G., Walbek, N. H., & Seely, R. K. (1987). Frequency of MMPI two-point code types among sex offenders. *Journal of Consulting and Clinical Psychology, 55*, 566-570. (Predominance of Pd and other patterns in sexually convicted prisoners.)

Friedman, A. F., Webb, J. T., & Lewak, R. (1989). Psychological assessment with the MMPI. Hillsdale, NJ: Lawrence Erlbaum Associates. (A good, detailed, basic text.)

Graham, J. R. (1990). MMPI-2: Assessing personality and psychopathology. New York, NY: Oxford University Press. (MMPI-2 revision co-author Graham's view of the MMPI-2.)

Greene, R. L. (1987). Ethnicity and MMPI performance: A review. Journal of Consulting and Clinical Psychology, 55, 497-512. (Major journal article showing the lack of consistent differences on the MMPI between white, black, Hispanic, Asian, and Native American samples.)

Greene, R. L. (1991). The MMPI-2/MMPI: An interpretive manual. Boston: Allyn & Bacon. (The best, current introductory text, although Friedman, Webb, and Lewak is close in quality and comprehensiveness.)

Greene, R. L. (1988). The MMPI: Use with specific populations. Philadelphia, PA: Grune & Stratton. (Ten topical chapters including pain, substance abuse, neuropsychological dysfunction, and child and sexual abuse; more current than the 1975 Dahlstrom, Welsh, & Dahlstrom Handbook, Vol. II.)

Hafner, A. J., Butcher, J. N., Hall, M. D., & Quast, W. (1969). Parent personality and childhood disorders: A review of MMPI findings. Chapter in: MMPI: Research developments and clinical applications, Butcher, J. N. New York: McGraw-Hill Book Company. (An extensive review of MMPI research up to 1969 on parent MMPI profiles vis-a-vis childhood psychopathology.)

Hathaway, S. R., & McKinley, J. C. (1943). *The Minnesota Multiphasic Personality Schedule.* Minneapolis, MN: University of Minnesota Press. (The original Manual for the MMPI; revised in 1951 as: Hathaway, S. R., & McKinley, J. C. *The Minnesota Multiphasic Personality Inventory Manual,* New York: Psychological Corporation.)

Keller, L. S., & Butcher, J. N. (1991). Assessment of chronic pain patients with the MMPI-2. Minneapolis, MN: University of Minnesota Press. (A discussion of pain research on the MMPI and MMPI-2.)

Meehl, P. E. (1954). Clinical versus statistical prediction: a theoretical analysis and a review of the evidence. Minneapolis: University of Minnesota Press.

Monahan, J., & Steadman, H. J. (Eds.) (1994). Violence and mental disorder: Developments in risk assessment. Chicago: The University of Chicago Press.

END OF PSYCHOLOGICAL REFERENCES

MMPI/MMPI-2 TESTIMONY AND APPEALABLE ISSUES

Stuart Greenberg, Ph.D., A.B.P.P.

The MMPI has been an issue on appeal in over 350 state court matters. What are some typical appeal issues?

> You must be competent in the use of a test in order to testify about the results of an administration of that test. (*West v. Martin, 1986*) [1]

> Non-psychologist physicians who are competent to interpret the test may do so in testimony. (*DeHaven v. Gant*, 1986) [2], (*Hagen v. Swenson,* 1975) [3], and (*People v. Cooper,* 1978) [4].

> A psychologist may use computer analysis of psychological tests as a basis for opinion but, absent a showing of reliability of computer results, they may not be independently received in evidence. (*Sallis v. Lamansky, 1988*) [5].
> Individual MMPI items may be admitted as evidence. (*State of Washington v. Rice,* 1988) [6].

> Parts of the MMPI computer interpretation may be read into the record. (*Sullivan v. Fairmont Homes, Inc.*,1989) [7].

> The MMPI may not be used, in the absence of other evidence, to determine that an individual has a tendency toward alcoholism and thereby deny him a job (*Adkerson v. MK-Ferguson Co.,* 1991) [8] or terminate him from a job (*Pinger v. Behavioral Science Center, Inc.,* 1988) [9].

> A psychologist may rely in part on the MMPI as a basis for recommending the termination of parental

basis for recommending the termination of parental rights *(In Re: Adoption of Stunkard*, 1988) [10] and *(Scott v. Prince George's Co. Dept. of Social Services*, 1988) [11].

A psychologist may rely in part on an invalid MMPI as a basis for testimony. *(Hawk v. Hawk*, 1990) [12].

The court is free to ignore the test results of an MMPI or any other test in reaching a conclusion. *(In re Complaint Concerning the Honorable Alberto O. Miera, 1988)* [13].

One psychologist may testify about the MMPI test results performed by another psychologist. *(Wesley v. State*, 1990) [14].

It is acceptable not to use the MMPI. *State of Maine v. Bridges* (1980) [15] and *In re L.M. III, a Minor v. Larry Mikel II, v. In re C.L.P., a Minor v. Larry Mikel II, In re C.P., D.M. and L.M. III, Minors, v. Serena Mik* (1985).

It is acceptable to ignore MMPI results if the results are not supported by the real-world test data. (*City of Greenwood v. Dowler*, 1985) [16].

The MMPI may be used as a partial basis for entering an insanity plea even though there is a normal range profile. *(State of Arizona v. McMurtrey*, 1986) [17].

Legal References

Stuart Greenberg, Ph.D., A.B.P.P.

1. West v. Martin, 11 Kan App 2d 55,713 P2d 957 (1986).

2. DeHaven v. Gant, 42 Wash.App. 666, 713 parent.2d 149 (1986).

3. Hagen v. Swenson, 236 N.W. 2d 161 (1975), (Supreme Court of Minnesota).

4. People v. Cooper, 64 Ill. App.3d 880, 381 N.E.2d 1178 (1978).

5. Sallis v. Lamansky, 420 NW2d 795 (Iowa 1988).

6. State of Washington v. Rice, 110 Wash.2d 577,757 parent.2d 889 (1988).

7. Sullivan v. Fairmont Homes, Inc., 543 N.E.2d 1130 (1989), (Court of Appeals of Indiana).

8. Adkerson v. MK-Ferguson Co., MichCtApp, No. 120434, 12/16/91, 58 Empl. Prac. December. parent 41, 401, 1919 Mich.App. 129,477 N.W.2d 465 (1991).

9. Pinger v. Behavioral Science Center, Inc., 52 Ohio App.3d 17, 566 N.E.2d 209 (1988)

10. InRe: Adoption of Stunkard, 551 A.2d 253 (Pa.Super. 1988).

11. Scott v. Prince George's Co. Dept. of Social Services, 76 Md.App. 347, 545   A.2d 81 (1988).

12. Hawk v. Hawk, 1990 WL 253036 (Ohio App.) (1990).

13. In re Complaint Concerning the Honorable Alberto O. Miera, 426 N.W.2d 850 (1988).

92

14. <u>Wesley v. State, 575 So.2d 108 (1990), (Court of Criminal Appeals of Alabama).</u>

15. <u>State of Maine v. Bridges, 413 A.2d 937 (1980).</u>

16. <u>City of Creenwood v. Dowler, 492 N.E.2d 1081 (1986), (Court of Appeals of Indiana, First District)</u>

17. <u>State of Arizona v. Mc.Murtrey, 151 Ariz. 105, 726 parent.2d 202 (1986).</u>

APPENDIX

MMPI/MMPI-2 PROFILES

MMPI/MMPI-2 CODING

The basic profile for the MMPI

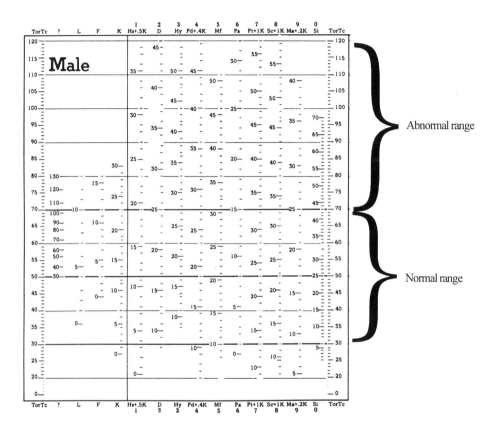

The "T-scores" are relative to a mean of 50 and a standard deviation of plus or minus 10. The raw scores are the count of how many items were answered in the significant or scored direction on that scale. Plus and minus two standard deviations was considered to be within the normal range.

The basic profile for the MMPI-2

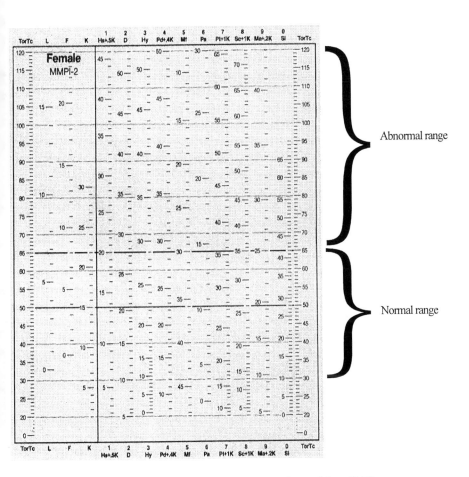

Note that the boundary for the abnormal range was changed from T-70 to T-65 on the MMPI-2. At T-70 on the MMPI-2, too many patients had "normal range" profiles.

THE "MMPI CODE"

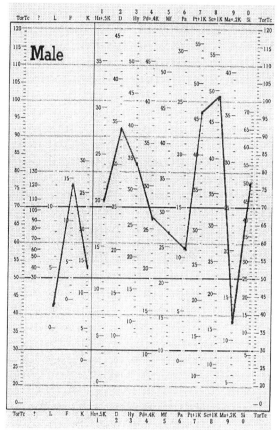

Code: 872*3"01'45-6/:9

The typewriter key symbols are inserted to indicate standard deviations as follows:

T-score: Symbol:

90+	*
80-89	"
70-79	'
60-69	-
50-59	/
40-49	:
30-39	#

29 or less to right of #

The scales are rank-ordered and the symbols reflect levels of elevation (the numbers for the scales precede the corresponding symbols). If the highest ranking scale is less than T-70, then the * for 90 and the " for 80 are omitted.

THE "MMPI-2 CODE"

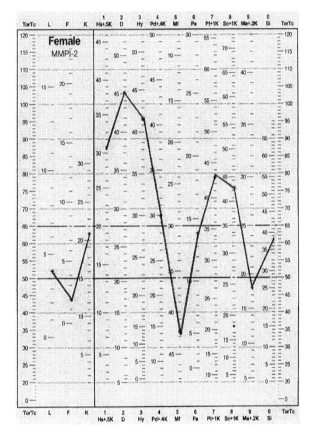

Code: 2**3*1"78'4+60-/9:5

The typewriter key symbols for the MMPI-2 were modified to be as follows (T-scores precede the symbols):

T-score: Symbol:

100+	**	(optional)
90-99	*	
80-89	"	
70-79	'	
65-69	+	(optional)
60-64	-	
50-59	/	
40-49	:	
30-39	#	

29 or less to right of #

As with the MMPI profile, the scales are rank-ordered and the symbols reflect levels of elevation (the numbers for the scales precede the corresponding symbols). If the highest ranking scale is less than T-70, then the * for 90 and the " for 80 are omitted.

INDEX